PRESENTED BY

Sam & Dora Unruh

The
Orthodox
Evangelicals

The Orthodox Evangelicals

Who they are and what they are saying

Edited by: **Robert E. Webber**
Donald Bloesch

THOMAS NELSON INC., PUBLISHERS
Nashville   **New York**

Library of Congress Cataloging in Publication Data
Main entry under title.

The orthodox evangelicals.

1. Evangelicalism—United States—Addresses, essays, lectures. 2. Theology, Doctrinal—Addresses, essays, lectures. I. Webber, Robert. II. Bloesch, Donald G., 1928–
BR1642.U5077   269'.2'0973   78–16124
ISBN 0–8407–5654–2

Contents

Preface

In May of 1977 a significant group of forty-five evangelicals gathered near Chicago to issue a Call to evangelicalism. The essential feature of the statement issued on that occasion was to call evangelicals back to historic Christianity.

THE ORTHODOX EVANGELICALS introduces that groundbreaking event to the general public, and sets forth an agenda for evangelical accomplishment in the last two decades of the twentieth century.

The Editors
June, 1978

I. Introduction

1. The Chicago Call:
An Appeal to Evangelicals

Prologue

In every age the Holy Spirit calls the church to examine its faithfulness to God's revelation in Scripture. We recognize with gratitude God's blessing through the evangelical resurgence in the church. Yet at such a time of growth we need to be especially sensitive to our weaknesses. We believe that today evangelicals are hindered from achieving full maturity by a reduction of the historic faith. There is, therefore, a pressing need to reflect upon the substance of the biblical and historic faith and to recover the fullness of this heritage. Without presuming to address all our needs, we have identified eight of the *themes to which we as evangelical Christians must give careful theological consideration.*

A Call to Historic Roots and Continuity

We confess that we have often lost the fullness of our Christian heritage, too readily assuming that the Scriptures and the Spirit make us independent of the past. In so doing, we have become theologically shallow, spiritually weak, blind to the work of God in others and married to our cultures.

Therefore we call for a recovery of our full Christian heritage. Throughout the church's history there has existed an evangelical impulse to proclaim the saving, unmerited grace of Christ, and to reform the church according to the Scriptures. This impulse appears in the doctrines of the ecumenical councils, the piety of the early fathers, the Augustinian theology of grace, the zeal of the monastic reformers, the devotion of the practical mystics and the scholarly integrity of the Christian humanists. It flowers in the biblical fidelity of the Protestant Reformers and the ethical earnestness of the Radical Reformation. It continues in the efforts of the Puritans and Pietists to complete and perfect the Reformation. It is reaffirmed in the awakening movements of the 18th and 19th centuries which joined Lutheran, Reformed, Wesleyan and other evangelicals in an ecumenical effort to renew the church and to extend its mission in the proclamation and social demonstration of the Gospel. It is present at every point in the history of Christianity where the Gospel has come to expression through the operation of the Holy Spirit: in some of the strivings toward renewal in Eastern Orthodoxy and Roman Catholicism and in biblical insights in forms of Protestantism differing from our own. We dare not move beyond the biblical limits of the Gospel; but we cannot be fully evangelical without recognizing our need to learn from other times and movements concerning the whole meaning of that Gospel.

A Call to Biblical Fidelity

We deplore our tendency toward individualistic interpretation of Scripture. This undercuts the objective character of biblical truth, and denies the guidance of the Holy Spirit among his people through the ages.

Therefore we affirm that the Bible is to be interpreted in keeping with the best insights of historical and literary study, under the guidance of the Holy Spirit, with respect for the historic understanding of the church.

We affirm that the Scriptures, as the infallible Word of God, are the basis of authority in the church. We acknowledge that God uses the Scriptures to judge and to purify his Body. The church, illumined and guided by the Holy Spirit, must in every age interpret, proclaim and live out the Scriptures.

A Call to Creedal Identity

We deplore two opposite excesses: a creedal church that merely recites a faith inherited from the past, and a creedless church that languishes in a doctrinal vacuum. We confess that as evangelicals we are not immune from these defects.

Therefore we affirm the need in our time for a confessing church that will boldly witness to its faith before the world, even under threat of persecution. In every age the church must state its faith over against heresy and paganism. What is needed is a vibrant confession that excludes as well as includes, and thereby aims to purify faith and practice. Confessional authority is limited by and derived from the authority of Scripture, which alone remains ultimately and permanently normative. Nevertheless, as the common insight of those who have been illumined by the Holy Spirit and seek to be the voice of the "holy catholic church," a confession should serve as a guide for the interpretation of Scripture.

We affirm the abiding value of the great ecumenical creeds and the Reformation confessions. Since such statements are historically and culturally conditioned, however, the church today needs to express its faith afresh, without defecting from the truths apprehended in the past. We need to articulate our witness against the idolatries and false ideologies of our day.

A Call to Holistic Salvation

We deplore the tendency of evangelicals to understand salvation solely as an individual, spiritual and otherworldly matter to the neglect of the corporate, physical and this-worldly implication of God's saving activity.

Therefore we urge evangelicals to recapture a holistic view of salvation. The witness of Scripture is that because of sin our relationships with God, ourselves, others and creation are broken. Through the atoning work of Christ on the cross, healing is possible for these broken relationships.

Wherever the church has been faithful to its calling, it has proclaimed personal salvation; it has been a channel of God's healing to those in physical and emotional need; it has sought justice for the oppressed and disinherited; and it has been a good steward of the natural world.

As evangelicals we acknowledge our frequent failure to reflect this holistic view of salvation. We therefore call the church to participate fully in God's saving activity through work and prayer, and to strive for justice and liberation for the oppressed, looking forward to the culmination of salvation in the new heaven and new earth to come.

A Call to Sacramental Integrity

We decry the poverty of sacramental understanding among evangelicals. This is largely due to the loss of our continuity with the teaching of many of the Fathers and Reformers and results in the deterioration of sacramental life in our churches. Also, the failure to appreciate the sacramental nature of God's activity in the world often leads us to disregard the sacredness of daily living.

Therefore we call evangelicals to awaken to the sacramental implications of creation and incarnation. For in these doctrines the historic church has affirmed that God's activity is manifested in a material way. We need to recognize that the grace of God is mediated through faith by the operation of the Holy Spirit in a notable way in the sacraments of baptism and the Lord's Supper. Here the church proclaims, celebrates and participates in the death and resurrection of Christ in such a way as to nourish her members throughout their lives in anticipation of the consummation of the kingdom. Also, we should remember our biblical designation as "living epistles," for here the sacramental character of the Christian's daily life is expressed.

A Call to Spirituality

We suffer from a neglect of authentic spirituality on the one hand, and an excess of undisciplined spirituality on the other hand. We have too often pursued a superhuman religiosity rather than the biblical model of a true humanity released from bondage to sin and renewed by the Holy Spirit.

Therefore we call for a spirituality which grasps by faith the full content of Christ's redemptive work: freedom from the guilt and power of sin, and newness of life through the indwelling and outpouring of his Spirit. We affirm the centrality of the preaching of the Word of God as a primary means by which his Spirit works to renew the church in its corporate life as well as in the individual lives of believers. A true spirituality will call for identification with the suffering of the world as well as the cultivation of personal piety.

We need to rediscover the devotional resources of the whole church, including the evangelical traditions of Pietism and Puritanism. We call for an exploration of devotional practice in all traditions within the church in order to deepen our relationship both with Christ and with other Christians. Among these resources are such spiritual disciplines as prayer, meditation, silence, fasting, Bible study and spiritual diaries.

A Call to Church Authority

We deplore our disobedience to the Lordship of Christ as expressed through authority in his church. This has promoted a spirit of autonomy in persons and groups resulting in isolationism and competitiveness, even anarchy, within the body of Christ. We regret that in the absence of godly authority, there have arisen legalistic, domineering leaders on the one hand and indifference to church discipline on the other.

Therefore we affirm that all Christians are to be in practical submission to one another and to designated leaders in a church under the Lordship of Christ. The church, as the people of God, is called to be the visible presence of Christ in the world. Every Christian is called to active priesthood in worship and service through exercising spiritual gifts and ministries. In the church we are in vital union both with Christ and with one another. This calls for community with deep involvement and mutual commitment of time, energy and possessions. Further, church discipline, biblically based and under the direction of the Holy Spirit, is essential to the well-being and ministry of God's people. Moreover, we encourage all Christian organizations to conduct their activities with genuine accountability to the whole church.

A Call to Church Unity

We deplore the scandalous isolation and separation of Christians from one another. We believe such division is contrary to Christ's explicit desire for unity among his people and impedes the witness of the church in the world. Evangelicalism is too frequently characterized by an ahistorical, sectarian mentality. We fail to appropriate the catholicity of historic Christianity, as well as the breadth of the biblical revelation.

Therefore we call evangelicals to return to the ecumenical concern of the Reformers and the later movements of evangelical renewal. We must humbly and critically scrutinize our respective traditions, renounce sacred shibboleths, and recognize that God works within diverse historical streams. We must resist efforts promoting church union-at-any-cost, but we must also avoid mere spiritualized concepts of church unity. We are convinced that unity in Christ requires visible and concrete expressions. In this belief, we welcome the development of encounter and cooperation within Christ's church. While we seek to avoid doctrinal indifferentism and a false irenicism, we encourage evangelicals to cultivate increased discussion and cooperation, both within and without their respective traditions, earnestly seeking common areas of agreement and understanding.

ORIGINAL SIGNERS OF THE CHICAGO CALL*

Marvin W. Anderson, *Bethel Theological Seminary*
John S. Baird, *University of Dubuque Theological Seminary*
Donald G. Bloesch, *University of Dubuque Theological Seminary*
Jon E. Braun, *New Covenant Apostolic Order*

*The signer's employing institutions are included for descriptive purposes only; the inclusion of these institutions does not indicate either their explicit or implied approval of the call.

Virgil Cruz, *University of Dubuque Theological Seminary*
James Daane, *Fuller Theological Seminary*
Donald W. Dayton, *North Park Theological Seminary*
Jan P. Dennis, *Good News Publishers*
Lane T. Dennis, *Good News Publishers*
Gerald D. Erickson, *Trinity College, Deerfield, IL*
Isabel A. Erickson, *Tyndale House Publishers*
Donald C. Frisk, *North Park Theological Seminary*
Pete Gillquist, *Thomas Nelson Publishers*
Alfred A. Glenn, *Bethel College*
Nathan Goff, *Pastor, College Church, Wheaton, IL*
Jim Hedstrom, *Student, Vanderbilt University*
Richard Holt, *D.D.S., Wheaton, IL*
Thomas Howard, *Gordon College*
Morris A. Inch, *Wheaton College*
Herbert Jacobsen, *Wheaton College*
Kenneth Jensen, *New Covenant Apostolic Order*
Kathryn Lindskoog, *Author*
Theodore Laesch, *Pastor, St. John Lutheran Church, Wheaton, IL*
Howard Loewen, *Mennonite Brethren Bible College*
Richard Lovelace, *Gordon-Conwell Theological Seminary*
F. Burton Nelson, *North Park Theological Seminary*
Ray Nethery, *Grace Haven Farm, Mansfield, Ohio*
Roger Nicole, *Gordon-Conwell Theological Seminary*
Victor R. Oliver, *Vice President, Haggai Institute, Atlanta, GA.*
M. Eugene Osterhaven, *Western Theological Seminary*
Lois M. Ottaway, *Wheaton College news service*
Gordon W. Saunders, *Trinity College, Deerfield, IL*
Rudolf Schade, *Elmhurst College*
Luci N. Shaw, *Harold Shaw Publishers*
Kevin N. Springer, *Graduate Student, University of Michigan*
Jeffrey N. Steenson, *Student, Harvard University Divinity School*
Donald Tinder, *Christianity Today*
Benedict Viviano, O.P., *Aquinas Institute of Theology*
Gordon Walker, *Pastor, Grace Fellowship Church, Nashville, TN*
Robert E. Webber, *Wheaton College*

Matthew Welde, *Presbyterians United for Biblical Concerns*
Lance Wonders, *Student, University of Dubuque Theological Seminary*

May 3, 1977

2. Behind the Scenes: A Personal Account

by
ROBERT WEBBER

Robert Webber, who was chairman of the Chicago Call, is Associate Professor of Theology at Wheaton College, Wheaton, Illinois. He received a Th.D. in Historical Theology from Concordia Theological Seminary and is the author of several books including Common Roots: A Call To Evangelical Maturity *(Grand Rapids: Zondervan, 1978).*

The gathering of evangelicals in May of 1977 to draft the Chicago Call was a climactic point in the spiritual journey of many of us. In the past ten years or so, a number of evangelicals have been growing beyond the borders of what has, until now, been regarded as the limits of evangelicalism. In the same way that our current evangelical fathers, Billy Graham, Harold Ockenga, Harold Lindsell, C. F. H. Henry, and others grew beyond the borders of fundamentalism, so we, following their example, have continued to look beyond present limitations toward a more inclusive and ultimately more historic Christianity.

In this sense we take very little, if any, issue with the doctrines of our current fathers. We can affirm that we, as twentieth-century evangelicals, stand in continuity not only with the evangelicalism of the seventies, the sixties, the fifties, and the forties, but also with the fundamentalism of the thirties and the twenties.

What is happening to us is analogous to the growth process. The adult still has the same identity as when a child, but the child has grown outside of himself. So we are still evangelicals, but evangelicals in the process of growing out of our previous narrow strictures. The Chicago Call and the people who framed it represent this process of change. The underlying essence of the Call and the firm commitment of its writers is to evangelical Christianity. But the writers of the Call recognize the theological weaknesses of evangelicalism and thus appeal to evangelicals to enlarge the borders of their faith. This enlargement will be accomplished by a more expansive reach into the witness of the church in history and a more inclusive attitude toward the various forms of the church in today's world.

Because this process of expansion characterizes the framers of the Chicago Call as well as the content of the Call itself, let me give a brief personal account of my own pilgrimage (as an example of what others may have gone through) as well as some personal insights into the way the Chicago Call actually took shape.

In 1965 I was a graduate student in New Testament studies at Concordia Theological Seminary in St. Louis. At that time graduate students were required to have two minors. I chose systematic theology as my first minor and historical theology as my second.

My first course in historical theology was on the "Apostolic Fathers." I didn't know what to expect since my own previous seminary education had been very weak in church history, and about the only contact I had had with patristics was in the area of Scripture and canon.

To my surprise the study of these Fathers revolutionized my thinking. To begin with it challenged the opinion I had held that a knowledge of the New Testament was sufficient, and that the study of the church and her theologians was at best an exercise in academic antiquity. I began to see for the first time that it was as foolish to skip over the life of the church in the world as it would be to ignore the history of Israel in the Old Testament. God was God in history, not only in biblical times, but also in the ongoing life of the church.

Furthermore, the study of the early Fathers raised the question of continuity. I had blindly assumed that my own brand of Christianity was clearly apostolic. But when I saw what the apostolic Fathers thought, I began to realize that my own faith and practice were not *exactly* in tune with that of the second century. Could it be, I asked, that the early Fathers had actually strayed that quickly from the New Testament? In some ways, perhaps, I had to answer yes. But what about other areas where my practice was lacking and not quite as full as what I was seeing in the early church? Could it be, I wondered, that my faith suffered from a kind of reductionism?

My second course was "Bibliography and Methodology of Historical Theology" under Carl S. Meyer, then dean of the graduate school and chairman of the department of historical theology. My fascination with the material must have become obvious to Dr. Meyer. At the end of the course he took me aside and said, "You're in the wrong major, Bob. You should be doing your doctorate in historical theology."

"Give me a good reason to switch majors?" I asked.

"I'll give you one good reason that I want you to think about seriously," Dr. Meyer said. "Evangelicals have numerous good scholars in the area of New Testament but almost none in the area of historical theology. If evangelicalism is to mature she is going to have to develop an interest in history, and this will come from trained historical theologians teaching in evangelical institutions. I simply think you can do much more for evangelicals in the area of history than you can by going on with your studies in New Testament."

Three months later I was a major in historical theology.

My own interest in historical theology centered on the Reformation and beyond, and it was in this area that I finished my degree. However, during my last ten years of teaching at Wheaton College, I have become progressively more interested in the Fathers of the church and in the strong theological foundations they laid. In the first place I came to realize that the Reformation was firmly rooted in the insights of the Fathers. My doctoral thesis on William Perkins was as much a study of Perkins's love of the Fathers as it was a study of Perkins himself. It gradually dawned on me that I could not really understand the Reformers until I had a firm grasp of the classical theology of the early church.

My interest in the Fathers was also heightened by my students. I noticed the immense interest they took in the Fathers when I spoke about them in class. It was significantly more than a casual interest. It was as though they had found some really significant roots—roots that did more than confirm their faith. They were challenged and stretched by the insights of the Fathers and felt that in these earliest thinkers of the church were leaders who could offer them positive insights and a faith that clearly articulated their gut-level feelings and concerns.

Organizing the Planning Committee

Gradually, I became aware of the fact that I was not the only one with these concerns. I heard of the interest being expressed at other evangelical schools, institutions, and organizations. One day in November of 1976, Peter Gillquist (editor at Thomas Nelson Publishers), who also shares concern for a more significant return to historic Christianity by evangelicals, called me to talk about our mutual interests. We both mentioned many others who shared our interest and for the first time I realized that a grass-roots movement toward a more traditional shape of the faith was actually emerging.

In the course of the conversation I said to Pete, "I think a conference of these people should be gathered for the purpose of giving a unified voice to these issues."

Pete replied, "If one is called, count me in."

Immediately after hanging up the phone, something inside of me said, "Why not, it's now or never . . . do it." I sat down immediately and penned the following words to Donald Bloesch, Peter Gillquist, and Thomas Howard:

> I think you agree with me that the time has come for evangelicals who are concerned for historic Christianity to meet together for prayer, discussion and action.
>
> For that reason I'm asking you to join with me to constitute a planning committee for a National Conference of Evangelicals for Historic Christianity to meet in the fall of 1977.
>
> The purpose of the conference is to bring together evangelical leaders to hammer out a brief declaration calling evangelicals to return to the historic faith and to discuss further ways and means of making an impact on the evangelical sub-culture to move it toward an affirmation of a truly catholic faith.
>
> As I see it, our responsibility on the steering committee would be to (1) determine when and where to meet, (2) set forth an agenda and (3) decide who should be invited. To give you some idea of what I have in mind I've enclosed a proposed agenda for the conference.
>
> My own feeling is that our purpose should revolve around a summary statement, a *call*, you might say, to historic Christianity. It should be inclusive of our major concerns, but brief. Also, I think only those persons who are both committed to the historic faith and are in positions of leadership and influence should be involved. It would probably be desirable to draw from all regions of the U.S. as well as from a number of different denominations.

It soon became apparent that it would be impossible to put the conference together with three other committee members who lived such a long distance from each other and whose schedules were too full to permit frequent meetings and brainstorming. The realization that we needed an executive committee forced me to look within my own church where there was a small cadre of young men and women who were exceptionally aware of the issues and were eminently qualified to provide leadership in calling such a conference. These persons were Lane Dennis, a doctoral student at Northwestern University; his brother Jan Dennis of Lithocolor Press; Gerald Erickson, professor of English at Trinity College in Deerfield; Isabel Erickson, book editor at Tyndale House; Victor Oliver, then editor in chief of Tyndale House; and Richard Holt, a dentist in Wheaton.

Organizing the Call

This little group of people (along with Donald Bloesch who frequently came for Saturday meetings from Dubuque, Iowa) began to meet on a regular basis to discuss, pray, and wait on the leading of God's Spirit. As I think again about these meetings I cannot recall a spirit of negative criticism or cynicism dominating these meetings in any way. We were all united in the conviction that evangelical Christianity was suffering from a reduction of the historic faith and practice. But our concern was always to offer something positive rather than to be mere critics of the evangelical movement. Furthermore, most of us by our vocations were firmly committed to evangelical institutions. We felt that we were speaking from inside the movement rather than from outside.

Our first major project was to discuss what we felt were the problems or weaknesses in evangelical Christianity. We brainstormed over such areas as church, ministry, and sacraments; Scripture, tradition, authority, and hermeneutics; worship, preaching, and music; theology; evangelism, education, and cross-cultural communication; ecumenism; social issues; spirituality; and seminary education.

In general we concluded that evangelicalism was suffering from two basic failures. First, an insufficient recognition of the implications of the Incarnation. Specifically, we felt that evangelicals were suffering from a kind of gnostic rejection of creation. We concluded that this failure to affirm the visible as "good" and as a "means through which God communicates Himself in saving grace to mankind" is evident in the low view evangelicals have of the church, worship, sacraments, and ministry. The corrective, we felt, would be found in a return to an incarnational view of theology. Second, we agreed that evangelicals were failing to recognize their continuity with the church in history. This is evident in the fact that many evangelicals pay little or no attention to church history or to the traditions of the church. And even those who do have a concern for church history usually trace their roots back only as far as the Reformation with a near disregard for everything that happened in the church up to that time (except perhaps for consideration of the Nicene Creed and a few of the Fathers).

A major concern that emerged in these discussions was to what extent our emphasis on the early church (the Fathers and catholicity) could be inclusive of the Reformers. Our small committee was somewhat divided on this issue. Some felt that the Reformation represented a departure from the early church in the areas of church, ministry, and sacraments. Others felt that the true spirit of the Reformation was catholic and that the departure from a true catholicity was more the result of the Enlightenment. In the midst of this discussion a crucial letter came from Jim Hedstrom (a doctoral student at Vanderbilt University and a participant in the conference) in which he effectively argued that "to recover catholicity we do not have to jettison our Protestant heritage, but exactly *recover it in its finest models.*"* After a brief discussion of Calvin's catholicity, Jim went on to argue:

> Many other examples could be drawn from our Protestant forbearers to support this contention, which to working historians should be no contention at all, but the simple truth. It was one of the tragedies of modern ecclesiastical history that the Oxford Movement felt it necessary to despise the Reformation, to achieve catholicity. Subsequent scholarship has shown that the view of the Protestant movement held by leading Tractarians was very defective, and has suggested that if Oxford men had lived a bit later, in the light of a rediscovered Luther and Calvin interest, their position might have been much modified in favor of the Protestant tradition. For those of us who *do* stand this side of modern Reformation study, it is altogether impossible to build a

*This letter and all other materials pertaining to the Call are housed in the archives of the Billy Graham Center, Wheaton, Illinois.

platform of catholic concern which ignores the genuine catholicity of Protestantism. This is a simple matter of scholarship and truth. But further, no emphasis upon catholicity among evangelicals especially is going to get anywhere by denying evangelical and reformed traditions, as these have had a genuinely catholic aspect. A movement which did this would be doomed from the outset to play the role of, not a reforming influence, but only a cult of private (I guess Anglo-Catholic) interest.

In this very discerning and spirited letter, Hedstrom went on to advocate caution against mere external changes that would adopt the trappings of catholicity:

Now I believe, of course, that an emphasis on catholicity can accord with the deepest aspirations of our own Protestant heritage. But we have to be very discerning in the way we approach, and voice, these concerns and intended reforms. We in no wise want to suggest that imposing certain externalisms is going to produce that *catholicity in spirit* which is the essence of our concern. Doing what culturally accommodated liberal or Neo-orthodox congregations have done, in taking in catholic trappings, can be a kind of death rite for declining evangelical churches. We're not advocating this! What we are advocating is the rediscovery of a catholic *comprehension,* which *may or may not* express itself today in some of the catholic forms of the past, *may or may not* find useful some of the historic modes of Christian worship and churchmanship. We must *be* catholic, in the inward man, before we can *act* catholic in formulating intelligently a program for our (to be reformed) evangelical communities. As you have mentioned in your letter, *prayer* is involved in this effort. This is a spiritual exercise of profound dimensions, and not a mechanical programmatics, where one can say "do this, and that will happen". We have here to do with meeting the Lord of the church, and His will for our collective future as evangelicals amid the currents of a greater Christian tradition and community. We need room for the Holy Spirit to lead us, and need to guard against assuming that we know *now* everything that needs to be done. The Lord leads a genuine reform one step at a time. My personal perception of this was behind my caution to you regarding perhaps waiting for a reaction to the book, before laying out a too formal program for all of your concerns. Let the Spirit have a chance to work, and perhaps bring some real participation into this. After all, if reform is to come, it will take a great host of people committed to the task, and this is not going to happen overnight.

The letter managed to put our divergent opinions into perspective and set us on a course that determined to bring together the Catholic, reformed, and evangelical perspectives.

Our next step was to outline the shape of the Call. Having spelled out the weaknesses we began next to set forth the correctives that we believed, if followed, would lead evangelicals back to a more historic faith. More than anything else this was a matter of organizing our concerns, finding proper headings, and arranging them in order of an inner dynamic. This matter of an inner sequential dynamic was crucial to us. We were all concerned with what we believed to be a "point theology" among evangelicals. By this I refer to a mere listing of doctrines, such as the inspiration of Scripture, the deity of Christ, and the substitutionary atonement as though they were "points" of theology that could stand or fall alone.

The organization of the Call therefore represents what we believe to be a sequential unfolding according to an inner dynamic. We placed "A Call to Historic Roots and Continuity" first because we felt that nothing else could change among evangelicals *until* there was a recovery of the past. As long as we exist in a narrow, isolated, and sectarian vacuum, there is no hope that we can be open to the broader and more inclusive scope of God's church in history.

This is true, for example, in the area of Scripture. The contemporary debate over inerrancy operates from a single model of Scripture and fails to take into account the significance of the authority of the Scripture *in the church*. Thus an appreciation of history provides us with a more adequate way to deal with the issue of authority and the problem of hermeneutics. We are to stand in a tradition and not in some isolated modern argument. This inner-connectedness reaches, then, from the call to the past all the way to a call to the future, namely, "A Call to Church Unity." Our concern was to

bring evangelicals back into the mainstream of the church:
past, present, and future.

An outline with suggested emphases was the fruit of our
discussion. It was sent to all the conferees *prior* to the confer-
ences so that they could see the direction we felt the conference
should take. The outline read as follows:

A suggested working outline for

THE CHICAGO CALL:

An Appeal to Evangelicals

In the planning committee's discussions, we have developed the following suggested structure and general
content of the call. We recognize, however, that the final
form of the call will be a product of the dynamics of the
conference, and will not exactly replicate this structure.

As shown on the suggested docket there will be both
sectional and plenary sessions. To help us organize the
conference, we need to have you indicate three areas of
most interest to you. Please do so on the enclosed pre-
registration form.

Prologue
Suggested emphasis:
—a general statement of the need for the call

1. A Call to Historic Roots and Continuity
Suggested emphases:
—return to apostolicity and catholicity
—recover pre-Reformation roots
—affirm the true insights of the historic reform movements

2. A Call to Biblical Fidelity
Suggested emphases:
—affirm a high view of Scripture (without error in all that it
affirms)
—recognize the biblical witness, illumined by the Spirit in

the church, as the basis of authority, and the crucial role of church traditions in the proclamation of this witness
—replace subjective hermeneutics with one that respects the objectivity of the unique revelation given in biblical history and conveyed through church traditions

3. A Call to Creedal Identity
Suggested emphases:
—affirm the normative value of the ecumenical creeds
—affirm the contextual value of confessional statements
—affirm the need for contemporary confessional witness

4. A Call to Holistic Salvation
Suggested emphases:
—affirm that the Atonement has as its object both the spiritual and the material creation and thus has implications for all of life
—recognize the corporate as well as the individual implications of salvation

5. A Call to Church Order
Suggested emphases:
—affirm the priesthood of all believers while recognizing also the diversity of callings
—recognize the community of faith as the continuing visible presence of Christ in the world
—affirm the necessity of biblical discipline and authority

6. A Call to Sacramental Integrity
Suggested emphases:
—recognize that creation and the Incarnation affirm the material world as both the object of and the vehicle for the creative activity of God's grace
—recognize the church as the primary environment in which the visible signs and means of grace operate through faith
—recognize the necessity of sacramental living

7. A Call to Spirituality
Suggested emphases:
—recognize the essentiality of and complimentary relationship between contemplative and active spirituality
—rediscover genuine prayer, discipline and worship
—restore the social and moral imperatives of the faith to their proper place within the church

8. A Call to Church Unity

Suggested emphases:

—reaffirm the basis of unity in fidelity to biblical and apostolic proclamation, worship and doctrine

—reject both mere spiritualization and the confederational concept of church unity

—work toward the visible witness and unity of the church in light of the Kingdom, present and future

Our next order of business was to determine who should be invited. Since we had already decided to try to achieve a statement that was catholic, reformed, and evangelical, there was little debate that those invited to the conference should reflect these traditions. Our *modus operandi* was to make a list of all evangelical schools and institutions and draw representative conferees from them. We purposefully invited people from the various traditions, such as Lutheran, Reformed, Anabaptist, and free church as well as Roman Catholic and Orthodox (no Orthodox representatives came). We wanted to see whether or not theologians and church leaders from these traditions could actually agree sufficiently enough to produce a call that was essentially catholic in spirit. In this sense we knew we were taking a risk. As a matter of fact, several members of the committee were certain that no consensus could be reached and that no statement would be forthcoming from such a divergent group.

The Conference Proceedings

When the conference convened, I think all members of the planning committee were a little nervous about what would happen. We had decided not to assume a strong role in the conference itself. We felt we had brought these people together to see whether or not a consensus could be reached, and that it would not be honest to attempt to manipulate the conferees into our agenda. The first challenge came when Don Tinder, associate editor of *Christianity Today,* questioned the proposed subtitle, "An Appeal To Evangelicals." He thought the word *Christians* should replace the word *Evangelicals.* We had actually spent hours discussing this very issue in our committee and concluded that the Call must be directed to a specific group to have an impact. An appeal to Christians in general, we felt, would simply be too nebulous. We were appealing to a specific group of Christians and not to *all* Christians. At first there seemed to be some support for Tinder's view. Actually, my heart sank for fear that the title might be changed. It would, in my opinion, have destroyed the whole appeal of the Call. After some discussion, the title the committee had chosen was accepted unanimously.

The second hurdle came with the discussion of the outline itself. A few questions were raised about the order, and "A Call to Church Order" was changed to "A Call to Church Authority." But other than these items, the conferees seemed satisfied with the proposed structure of the Call and approved the outline unanimously.

Following this the conferees gathered in the groups they had selected prior to the conference and began working on the statements for their sections. The initial conference document, a compilation of each group's work, was put together by early evening. It was reviewed in a plenary session after supper and the conferees agreed that it was particularly weak stylistically. Consequently, the planning committee suggested the final format of two paragraphs for each section, the first paragraph stating the problem and the second offering an answer—or at least a redirection in which an answer might be found. All the conferees returned to their small groups to rewrite the statements. Late that night the planning committee went through the entire rough draft ironing out particular difficulties and developing stylistic unity.

The next day in plenary session the entire assembly went through the draft word by word. The main contention throughout the day was between those who desired a more Catholic expression and those who wanted to retain a language more common to the Reformers. This issue became particularly evident in "A Call To Sacramental Integrity," which was sent back for rewriting before gaining approval. The conferees were in good spirits throughout the day, evidencing a real sincerity in seeking to understand other points of view. The statement was completed late in the day and signed by all but three of the conferees.

Reaction to the Call

A response to the Chicago Call occurred immediately in some of the major publications in the United States. *Newsweek* magazine took a strong interest in the Call and regarded it as pointing to a "significant drift" among evangelicals "toward more traditional forms of Christianity." They saw the Call as "an unprecedented appeal" urging evangelicals to achieve "full maturity" as Christians by abandoning their narrow "sectarian mentality." And the writers correctly recognized that the Call represented the fact that some evangelicals were "dissatisfied with their inherited identities as sacred Christians," and that "they hope to recover what their forefathers rejected."[1]

An editorial in *Christian Century* compared the writing of the Call to the beginnings of the Oxford Movement in England in the nineteenth century. Mentioning the fact that numerous calls and manifestos are coming forth today, and that most of them get dumped into the wastebasket, the writer went on to say "this 'Chicago Call,' however, we've lingered over and savored, for in it is a serious call to a devout and more ordered church life." The author concluded that "if the 'Call' draws response, it is possible that what people now call 'mainline' religion will be strengthened . . . at the very least, this kind of call will help conservative Protestants and some Catholics look into over-looked dimensions of faith and life, and that is all to the good."[2]

Christianity Today compared the Call with the Chicago Declaration and the Lausanne Covenant. "The Chicago Declaration challenged evangelicals to greater concern about the ills of society; the Lausanne Covenant focused on world evangelization. The Chicago Call supplements, rather than differs from, the others with an appeal to greater concern for more traditional "churchmanship." The writer went on to "endorse heartily" the giving of "careful theological consideration" to the issues set forth in the Call, and suggested that "where present practice is found to be out of keeping with biblical precept, let us 'be doers of the word, and not hearers only.' "[3]

Not everyone, however, greeted the Call with such favorable response. In a letter to *Christianity Today,* one concerned person warned against the Call's statement that Scripture must be interpreted "with respect for the historic understanding of the church." "Such folly," he argued, "will only serve the cause of scriptural disobedience under the guise of "interpretation with respect for tradition," and will sow the seeds of a new battle for the Bible some decades hence." Another respondent wondered, "Why there was not a more representative body which drafted the call," observing that "a group so unrepresentative of the church can be unrealistic if they are not careful."[4]

How to Read this Book

In a personal conversation with Harold Lindsell—then editor of *Christianity Today*—I asked him what he thought of the Call.

"It's good, it's really good," he said, "but it was put together by such a mixed bag."

Evangelical Christianity, properly understood, *is* a mixed bag. By bringing together the "mixed bag" the Chicago Call succeeded in drawing up a platform for a "maturing evangelicalism." We need to come to the place where we stop building walls, even within our own camp. Instead we need to search for the common basis from which we can not only work together, but begin to reach outside of ourselves toward Christendom in general. This, I believe, may be accomplished by regaining our past without in any way affecting our firm conviction that the Scriptures are the final source of our authority.

Nevertheless, we have not yet achieved that unity, even among those who drafted the Call. The contributions to this book evidence the fact that we have only begun our pilgrimage toward a more appreciative understanding of each other. Because the Call is a "consensus statement," it should be noted that the authors of each chapter write from their own particular background whether that be Catholic, Reformed, or more generally evangelical. For that reason it must be remembered that only the Call itself is representative of the entire group that met to call evangelicals to maturity. Each writer, therefore, represents his own point of view, and the reader must judge each writer individually and not treat the writing as representative of a "movement." In this way, both that which is "uniformly agreed upon," namely the Call, and the individual's approach to the corporate statement retain the integrity that belongs to each.

Of the forty-five scholars, pastors, theologians, and students who attended the Chicago Call meeting, only three found they were unable to sign the Call statement. One of them declined for reasons of prior commitment to a fraternal order whereby signing would tend to commit the whole order to the Chicago Call statement. Another feared that signing the statement would draw unpleasant reprisals from the institution he served. The third person declined to sign because he differed from the consensus of the other forty-three participants in the Call. His reasons for abstaining were as follows:

(1) He saw the Call as leaning toward Roman theology in certain of its statements. I personally differ with him on this. The Call is Catholic in that it seeks to revive the historic theology of the church—namely that which the church agreed upon in the centuries before it became distinctly Roman. The Reformers rebelled against the Roman take-over of the church in the fourteenth and fifteenth centuries, and sought to restore the insights of the Fathers. You might say that the framers of the Call were concerned about restoring those insights into the church that are both ancient and Reformational.

(2) He also felt that certain aspects of the Call, in particular the section on a "Call to Sacramental Integrity," leaned toward Eastern church orthodoxy. My own feeling is that the Eastern Orthodox church has developed some valid insights into spirituality, and they need not be rejected simply because they are

Orthodox. However, I rather doubt that anyone consciously drew from Orthodoxy. The emphasis was drawn more from the current recognition on the part of biblical scholars that the Christian faith is holistic having to do with the whole man. Thus, being and action are emphasized as central to spiritual growth.

(3) He felt that the Call tended to be soft on Scripture. It is true that we chose not to deal with the "inerrancy" issue. However, the reason this was done had nothing to do with a low view of Scripture. The concern was that the point of the Call be a return to historical appreciation. What we wanted to emphasize was the need to interpret Scripture in the context of the church's tradition as a means of showing that the authority of Scripture does not rest on inerrancy *alone.* The Scripture traditionally has been regarded as the supreme authority in the church. (This did not break down until the fourteenth and fifteenth century, and then, not universally.) The point is that there is a measure of strength in the recognition that the *church* has always held a high view of the Scripture. To go against that conviction is to go against the tradition of history. That cannot be taken lightly. And that was the point we wanted to make. In short, the framers' concern was to put together a statement that, drawing on the history of the church, was truly Catholic, Orthodox, Reformed, and Evangelical.

What We Hope the Call Will Do

It is a very difficult thing to state exactly what we hope the Chicago Call will effect in the church. But I can dream for a moment and state what I would like to see happen as a result of the Call. These points are not listed in any order of priority, but more as they come to mind.

First, I hope the Call will help to restore a sense of historical awareness among evangelical Christians. We are, for the most part, a people without roots. Some of us can only trace the beginnings of our denomination or church to some time in this century—arising out of a split over this or that doctrine, or maybe even a personality clash between two strong leaders. Most of us have no sense of the past, no understanding of where we came from or what our original concerns even were. A true sense of the whole church in history, and our "belongingness" to it, should result in a more inclusive spirit on our part. It will help to break down our divisive and somewhat judgmental temperament and make us more charitable, open, and loving toward others whose traditions we may not now understand. Furthermore, a renewed historical awareness will help us become more ecumenical in the true sense of the word. By understanding the historical occasion that stands behind every denomination including our own, we will become, hopefully, more concerned for unity and oneness as the goal of the church. I don't mean a mere organizational unity, but one in spirit and in anticipation of the ultimate unity of the body of Christ.

Secondly, I hope the Call will help restore the content of Christianity to evangelicals. We tend toward a superficiality, a pop-evangelicalism that markets Christ in the mass media. He's the cure for all ills—mental, physical, and social. I do not intend to demean the healing power of Christ; what is offensive is the rather simplistic and instant-cure formula that He has become. This is demeaning to Christ's person. It overlooks the complexity of man's problems and it by-passes the more in-depth, far-reaching implications of the Christian faith. For example, the healing that Christ brings into our broken lives is generally accomplished in the nurturing and healing context of the church and the sacraments. If we deny, both in doctrine and then in action, what the church is and what God can do and does in the church and by the sacraments, then we have cut ourselves off from the channels through which God continues to work in the world. By recovering the *content* of Christ, we will open ourselves to new ways to grow as well as discover new ways to serve. The specific content we want evangelicals to grapple with is outlined in the eight points of the Call. These are the areas of our greatest weakness.

Thirdly, I hope the Call will eventuate in a sense of community among evangelicals. We are really a very fragmented group—all of us going our own way. We have too heavy a dose of individualism in our midst. We tend to build our own empires and dogmatically rule our own little spheres. What we need is not only a common base, but the sense that we are moving toward the fulfillment of the base. I do not mean to deny the Trinitarian character of the church, i.e., unity within diversity. What I am hoping is that we can affirm and fulfill the Trinitarian character of the church. We have the diversity but lack the unity. Perhaps the Call can serve as an expression at least of our common concerns, and therefore provide us with the sense of community we so desperately need.

How Can These Changes Come About?

Now the question is *how*, by what means can this be accomplished? Naturally, we have no chain of command, so to speak, through which this can be channeled. What we need are *people* who will capture this vision and effect it in their places of influence. There are specifically three institutions through which this can be accomplished.

First, I would look to the schools—particularly our seminaries, Christian liberal arts colleges, and Bible colleges. What we need in these schools is a good dose of church history and historical theology. In the past our curriculums have paid scant attention to these disciplines, but in recent years, they have begun to come into their own. Students are hungry for the knowledge of the past, particularly the past of the church. We need young men and women to train in these areas, to catch the vision, and to enter these schools to inspire and train others.

Secondly, I look to our evangelical publishing houses. It's safe to say that much of the popular material published by evangelicals is lacking in solid content. The argument is that you have to publish what will sell. The point I want to make is that it is a matter of responsibility. People can only read what is published. We need to take more seriously the task of publishing good, solid reading material—literature that bears truthful content and makes us think. I am not against writing clearly and interestingly. What I am against is the blatant superficiality of our best sellers. Many of these books are offensive to the Christian gospel, and yet they bear the stamp of approval by virtue of their publication. We need a few fearless editors and publishers, along with a few writers who have some understanding of the problems we face and the direction given to these problems by the application of solid biblical principles. There is too much sugar-coated secular psychology passed off as gospel truth. And in too many of our books on the church we suffer from the desperate attempt to model a divine institution along the lines of a successful corporation. Somebody is going to have to stop this trend. Maybe the Call will help.

Finally, some people on the local level will have to catch the vision. If we really believe the principle of the priesthood of all believers, then the lay people of our churches must be allowed to speak and lead. What we need are some lay people who will refuse to allow their Christian sensibilities to be dulled by the reductionism of pop-evangelicalism. There are many intelligent lay people, elders, deacons, and ministers in the evangelical movement who know that the faith is deeper than the superficial image we give it. They are the ones who will have to stop buying the cheap books. They are the ones who will have to turn their backs to closed-mindedness, judgmentalness, and divisiveness. They will have to learn to stand up for a faith with content, and demand change. Perhaps the Call will provide them with the basis and be the means to strengthen their convictions.

My hope is that this book will help you understand the content of the Call better and provide you with a new vision of what it means to belong to Christ and His church.

Notes

1. *Newsweek,* 23 May 1977, p. 76.
2. *Christian Century,* 1 June 1977, p. 527.
3. *Christianity Today,* 17 June 1977, p. 27.
4. *Christianity Today,* 29 July 1977, p. 8.

II. An Explanation
of the Call

3. A Call to Historic Roots and Continuity

by

RICHARD LOVELACE

Richard Lovelace is Professor of Church History at Gordon-Conwell Theological Seminary in South Hamilton, Massachusetts. He is a graduate of Yale University and Westminster Seminary and holds the Th.D. in American Church History from Princeton Theological Seminary.

We confess that we have often lost the fullness of our Christian heritage, too readily assuming that the Scriptures and the Spirit make us independent of the past. In so doing, we have become theologically shallow, spiritually weak, blind to the work of God in others and married to our cultures.

Therefore we call for a recovery of our full Christian heritage. Throughout the church's history there has existed an evangelical impulse to proclaim the saving, unmerited grace of Christ, and to reform the church according to the Scriptures. This impulse appears in the doctrines of the ecumenical councils, the piety of the early fathers, the Augustinian theology of grace, the zeal of the monastic reformers, the devotion of the practical mystics and the scholarly integrity of the Christian humanists. It flowers in the biblical fidelity of the Protestant Reformers and the ethical earnestness of the Radical Reformation. It continues in the efforts of the Puritans and Pietists to complete and perfect the Reformation. It is reaffirmed in the awakening movements of the 18th and 19th centuries which joined Lutheran, Reformed, Wesleyan and other evangelicals in an ecumenical effort to renew the church and to extend its mission in the proclamation and social demonstration of the Gospel. It is present at every point in the history of Christianity where the Gospel has come to expression through the operation of the Holy Spirit: in some of the strivings toward renewal in Eastern Orthodoxy and Roman Catholicism and in biblical insights in forms of Protestantism differing from our own. We dare not move beyond the biblical limits of the Gospel; but we cannot be fully evangelical without recognizing our need to learn from other times and movements concerning the whole meaning of that Gospel.

The resurgence of the evangelical movement in American Christianity, widely noted by the press during the presidential campaign in the bicentennial year, appears to be a reality and not simply a media event. Certainly the last decade has involved a fairly large numerical multiplication of evangelical Christians in this country.

Problems in the Evangelical Resurgence

But there is still a question in the minds of many observers about how much more is involved beyond mere growth in numbers. Crime, social injustice, and cultural decay are still proceeding at a rate that casts doubt on the reality of the presence of large quantities of the salt of the earth within our society. New converts and newly awakened parishioners are enthusiastic and effusive, but not many show the effects of the deep conviction of sin and awareness of the glory of God characteristic of past "great awakenings." There are few places where fresh and powerful theological currents are flowing to accompany the numerical growth of evangelicalism.

All of this can readily be explained as the result of immaturity in the awakening movement. Evangelicalism has been growing rapidly since it began to reform its tradition in the 1940s, and it has reached an adolescent stage in which some of its latent powers are still undeveloped. The shaping and transformation of thought, society, and culture may still lie in the future.[1]

The image of adolescence seems to be an appropriate one for the spectacular leap in evangelical growth in the last few years, which has left the movement with multiple crises of identity. The observing world is confused by all the very diverse and even antithetical subcultures that call themselves evangelical, which make the whole movement easy to laud or defame according to one's bias and the part of the menagerie one is watching.

But even evangelicals themselves are not too sure of their identity. Some younger ones are no longer sure that it is helpful or necessary to distinguish themselves from other Christians by a party label. They are unaware of the reasons why their movement appeared within the church and have not asked whether or not its work is finished. Others are almost post-evangelical in their reaction against the perceived weaknesses of the movement. These have rarely grasped the essential genius of the movement that gave them birth, and they have not tried to distinguish between its ideal form and its accidental corruptions.

Research into the historical roots of evangelicalism is one of the most fruitful and illuminating methods of resolving the identity crisis of this movement. When the line of ancestry is traced back beyond "the Great Century" of missionary expansion to explore the Evangelical Awakening in the eighteenth century and the theological foundations of the movement in the sixteenth and seventeenth centuries, there is a strong infusion of content into the evangelical label, and also an opening of many avenues to other parts of the church's tradition that can broaden and deepen the evangelical experience today. An acquaintance with this heritage is a powerful impetus toward reformation and maturity, for there are many aspects of twentieth-century "revivalism" that the founders of the evangelical movement would judge to be seriously in need of revival.

Evangelicals themselves need to study their identity with critical rigor with the goal of recovering the fullness of their own tradition and reaching even beyond this toward a catholicity that surpasses anything in past evangelical experience. After the Second Awakening in England, the children of many evangelicals moved away from the movement their parents had founded to embrace the churchly traditionalism of the Tractarians and the spontaneity of early liberalism. There may have been faults in parents and children that help explain these mutations, but it is also possible that there was a narrowness and a partiality, a want of wholeness in the original movement that gave ground toward this secession. This process of mutation has occurred many times in the history of evangelicalism. It usually springs from a want of balance and catholicity that makes movements vulnerable to countermovements with a complementary imbalance. One of the best methods of promoting reconciliation between the fathers and the children in today's evangelicalism is to study the full identity of classical evangelicalism as revealed in its historical origins.

The Evangelical Impulse

What do we mean by the term "evangelical"? The name and the concept conveyed in the term go back to the Protestant Reformation, and might be identified with Philip Schaff's definition of "the Protestant principle," which involved as its formal element the supremacy of biblical authority, and as its material element the doctrine of justification by faith.[2] This would give us an evangelical lineage stretching back at least to 1517—embracing the main streams of Protestant orthodoxy;

some forms of Anabaptism; the Puritans; the Pietists; and the later prophets and leaders of evangelical revival.

It would appear that by Schaff's definition, as in common European usage, "evangelical" and "Protestant" were equivalent in meaning, and therefore that the evangelical heritage would be confined within Protestantism. But Schaff's genius as a church historian stemmed in large part from his refusal to accept the common Protestant assumptions that all vital Christianity began in the Reformation period, or was contained in hidden streams before the Reformation that anticipated the Protestant understanding of justification.

Schaff saw that the only Christianity historically visible before the Reformation was contained in the Western and Eastern Catholic traditions, and also that these traditions had contributed much of the foundation for Reformation faith. All modern church historians have followed him in this conclusion. This suggests that Schaff sensed a kind of "evangelical impulse" in many parts of pre-Reformation Christianity that were aiming toward the reformation and renewal of the church, even if these parts did not often achieve the full expression of this impulse. It is no accident that the Reformers were Christian humanists, that their Christology was orthodox according to the conciliar formulations, and that in so many instances they came out of monastic or ascetic backgrounds. They simply brought to full and balanced expression the evangelical impulse behind earlier persons and movements activated by the Holy Spirit in the early and medieval church. Explanding slightly Schaff's definition of the "Protestant Principle," we might define "the evangelical impulse" as *an urgent drive to proclaim the saving, unmerited grace of Christ, and to reform the church according to the Scriptures.*

Some readers may feel it would be clearer and more traditional simply to refer to a large circle of doctrine that is *catholic* and foundational, and that this larger circle of doctrine laid down by the early church contains a smaller concentric circle of strictly *evangelical* or Protestant doctrine added by the Reformers. This is an acceptable way of stating the case, but it does not emphasize quite as effectively the assertion that there is an organic unity between catholic and evangelical doctrines, persons, and movements, and the same Spirit-given impulse energizing these; so that *one cannot be authentically catholic without reaching beyond toward what is evangelical, nor can one be truly evangelical without recovering the fullness of what is catholic.*

The Evangelical Stream in the Early Church

We can see evidence for the truth of this statement in the strong if discriminating use of patristic materials by the Reformers to buttress their own arguments. It is quite obvious that the core of both Luther's and Calvin's theology is closely related to the great stream of Augustinian spirituality that dominated the Middle Ages, even though they explicitly rejected the superstructure the medieval scholastics built upon Augustine. The Puritans, eager to develop a distinctively Protestant spirituality, drew even more widely on the wisdom and piety of the early fathers, and were able to learn occasionally from Bernard and Thomas Aquinas. The early Protestant use of treasures in the storehouse of Catholicism was more than a matter of inertia in retooling the educational process; it was evidence of a sense of kinship with pre-Reformation Christianity, and a use and celebration of its products, which many Protestants, including evangelicals, no longer have today. Compared to our Protestant forebears, we have suffered a reduction of the historic faith.

Do these admissions constitute a retreat from the distinctive advances of Reformation Christianity, a high-church movement away from Protestantism? Emphatically not. Nothing in what has been said so far suggests that pastures are greener in the Catholic fold. There is an evident process in history through which the church has progressively understood and appropriated more and more of the truth of Christ set forth in Scripture. The Reformation rediscovered in the church's treasury the doctrine of justification by faith alone and other biblical truths.

What is needed today is not a movement away from Reformation principles and other biblical emphases that came into the church's possession during the evangelical awakenings, but simply a recovery of treasures that Protestantism has mislaid in its historical pilgrimage since the Reformation, combined with a pressing forward toward the full expression of the evangelical impulse. What follows is an inventory of the treasures contained in the storehouse of evangelical catholicity.

Prior to the Second Vatican Council, Catholic observers regarded their Protestant brethren somewhat in the way ocean-dwelling fish might look at their tiny cousins condemned to live in fishbowls. For Protestants, a better metaphor would involve the mutual observation of fish of equivalent size in separate landlocked ponds. As the Protestant mind views the development of early and medieval Catholicism in the East and the West, it does not find everything in these waters totally conducive to spiritual health. The most serious visible problem is probably the restriction of the Pauline understanding of grace by the collapsing of the concept of justification into sanctification and the performance of good works. By the early second century it is clear that Christians had come to think of themselves as being justified through being sanctified, accepted as righteous according to their actual obedience to the new Law of Christ.[3] The uneasy conscience created by this loss, compounded by a confusion of the mortification of sin with the amputation of whole areas of experience, gave rise to a luxuriant overgrowth of ascetic masochism. Luther commented that most of the deformities the Reformers found in medieval practice, and particularly the elevation of the clergy and the sacramental system into a mediatorial role, were generated by this restriction of the understanding of grace: "Ah, if the article on justification hadn't fallen, the brotherhoods, pilgrimages, masses, invocation of saints, etc., would have found no place in the church. If it falls again (which may God prevent!) these idols will return."[4]

But the most remarkable thing about the early church is the glory of its achievements in spite of its partial understanding of justification. Evangelicals today who doubt the regeneracy of church people who have not correctly grasped the Protestant doctrine of justification must blind themselves to the heroic witness of the early church under persecution. Fortified by a sharp challenge concerning the importance of godly living, its members were as ready to offer a praiseful witness through a martyr's death as to endure the slow martyrdom of ascetic spirituality. Cut off from the possibility of indulging in "cheap grace" by the church's bias toward legalism, the leaders became specialists in sanctification, and as a consequence their writings are filled with a real if not entirely balanced spiritual vitality.

The Protestant who is unable to learn and be edified through the brilliance of Tertullian and Clement of Alexandria or who fails to rejoice in the biblical solidity of Irenaeus or the eloquence of John Chrysostom is spiritually asleep. Today's Protestants rarely read this material except as they encounter it in the Puritans and the Reformers. It might be expected that nonevangelicals would therefore suffer the greatest loss in this respect since their theology is often rooted only in the last few decades of the twentieth century; but too often evangelical theology is not rooted more deeply than nineteenth-century redactions of Protestant orthodoxy, and thus never taps the reservoir of patristic wisdom in earlier Protestantism.[5]

The greatest stream of this wisdom is certainly the Augustinian tradition that is the crowning achievement of patristic theology and which continues to nourish both the Middle Ages and the Reformation. Probably no one should be permitted to practice theology who has not travelled through Augustine. His command of Scripture and of language matches those of Luther and Calvin, and he possesses a unique ability to reflect with love and delight upon the beauty and glory of God, even in the midst of polemic argument.

His Neoplatonism may interfere at some points with the biblical consistency of his theology, but it also reinforces this sense of the beauty of God, along with a mystical spirituality that is still basically evangelical in content. His sense of God's holiness and the depth of human sin is the deepest we encounter in the church before the Reformers. His philosophy of history, the doctrine of the Two Cities, remains the framework for the basic understanding of the church's redemptive task that distinguishes evangelical and Roman Catholic theologies from most others today.

Even where he takes a desperately wrong turn theologically, for instance when he concludes that the Donatists should be compelled to come into the church by the power of the magistrate, it is in the context of a sharp analysis of the danger of the extinction of charity in the process of schism. He explains justification as our acceptance by God resulting from an infusion of the sanctifying life of Christ that brings the believer into a state of grace; and he understands this process as the result of the unmerited kindness of God, grounded not upon works and merit but on a persevering dependence upon the mercy of Christ. It is true that he fuses his great understanding of Paul and the rest of Scripture with an acceptance of tradition and contemporary Catholic practice that is not sufficiently discerning. It is true that many of the features of modern Catholicism, which are most distressing to Protestants, along with many of the strongest currents in Protestant theology, are equally rooted in Augustine. But just for these reasons it is essential that both Protestants and Catholics go back to obtain an intimate acquaintance with his work, for it is the main crossroads of divergence between the two traditions, and it could also be the juncture at which unity might be regained.[6]

Protestant liberalism tended to dismiss the Christological subtleties of the ecumenical councils as an intrusion of Hellenic philosophy that distorted a basically Hebraic faith. But the magisterial Reformers built upon conciliar orthodoxy, and almost every biblically anchored theology since the Reformation has wrestled with the same issues that were before the councils. Athanasius' struggle against the denial of Christ's divinity is still relevant to evangelicals; so is his patient labor without separating from a church that remained officially Arian for decades.[7]

The Evangelical Impulse in Medieval Christianity

Asceticism within the early church is the source of the tradition of clerical celibacy that has remained one of the most problematic features in Roman Catholicism, both for Protestants and for Catholics with ministerial vocations. This should not prevent our recognition that the monastic movement was the cutting edge of reformation in the post-Constantinian church. The most vigorous leaders during the patristic era were converts to asceticism: Athanasius, who broadcast the Alexandrian ideal through his life of Anthony; the Cappadocian Brothers; Chrysostom; Jerome; Ambrose; and Augustine.

Those who entered the monastic movement and followed the moderate and careful rule of Benedict of Nursia were in effect strapping themselves into a sanctification machine; they were attacking the problems of pride and greed and lust by the radical surgery of obedience, poverty, and chastity. But who are we to say that they did not often attain the holiness they sought with such exaggerated stress? "Let not him who eats regard with contempt him who does not eat. . . . To his own master he stands or falls; and stand he will, for the Lord is able to make him stand" (Rom. 14:3,4; NASB).

The evidence indicates that despite their incomplete understanding of justification, they became the perennial source of reforming leaders and movements during decadent periods in the medieval church, the shock troops of missionary outreach, and the main preserving force both for Christian and non-Christian culture during the Middle Ages. In many instances the monasteries functioned not as decaying enclaves of retreat from the world, but as centers of renewal, models of Christian community, that publicly displayed at least one vision of the society of heaven and enriched the surrounding culture by their example of patient labor. They were the first Christian counterculture, and it is no accident that the Jesus Movement has produced communes that echo the monastic impulse toward ideal Christian fellowship.[8]

The Middle Ages is a difficult period for many evangelicals to appreciate. The fusion of church politics and imperial religiosity in this era produced a tangled mass of history with a disturbingly secular shape, despite the claims of "Christendom." Nevertheless, the attempt to impose Christian values on culture during this period produced results that are extremely instructive to us, both positively and negatively. Evangelicals have often sought to abstract their faith from art and culture because of fear of worldly contamination, and in doing this have sterilized their witness through the arts. But medieval culture produced enduring monuments pointing to its understanding of Christianity—in literature, painting, architecture, and music. To say that we should build temples made of living stones is not to deny the value of cathedrals; to seek the beauty of holiness is not to make a virtue of plainness.

Although the Protestant Reformation was grounded in a reaction against the scholastic theology that sought to fuse pagan philosophy with Augustinianism, we must not overlook the fact noted by Josef Pieper that this process of fusion in Albertus Magnus and Thomas Aquinas was a responsible attempt to come to terms with the Aristotelian wave of thought that was sweeping over Western society and threatening to paganize it while simultaneously unlocking its technical faculties. We should also recognize that the works of Anselm and Aquinas still have a great deal to teach us in the problems they raise and the painstaking care with which they pursue them, and sometimes also in the answers they offer.[9]

Medieval piety was directed toward a great variety of devotional objects and mediatorial persons. Protestants who understand the genius of their own tradition cannot help but conclude that much of this spirituality was (to echo T. E. Hulme's definition of Romanticism) "spilt religion," a devotion that has overflowed the Trinitarian channels within which it should properly flow and has moved into idolatry. Prayer to the saints and other superstitious relics of medieval faith still present in popular Catholicism are among the most serious standing scandals in modern Christianity, and we must continue to make a firm and deliberate plea that these be reformed. Nevertheless, there is a treasury of authentic Christian spirituality present in the writings of Bernard, Bonaventure, the Victorine theologians, and other medieval authors that ought to be shared among the whole church.[10]

The mystical tradition, with its characteristic ladder of ascent toward God (purgation of sin, illumination, followed by union) exactly reverses the Protestant understanding of fellowship with God (union with Christ by faith, illumination by the Spirit, and then the process of overcoming sin through growth in sanctification). The Protestant understanding of the centrality of faith in spiritual life is antithetical to ladders by which we must climb our way toward God.

Still there is no doubt that *in practice* the "triple way" of practical mysticism did bring a great many people into intimate communion with God, and that *in practice* it offers a challenge to work at maintaining fellowship with the Spirit of Christ that is much needed among indolent Protestants. The work of practical mystics like John Tauler, Thomas à Kempis, Brother Lawrence, and the *Devotio Moderna* is still a precious deposit of spiritual wisdom that the modern church should use. It is no accident that Luther felt himself indebted to Tauler; the Dominican had little use for scholastic theology and the calculus of merits, and he gave no wrong answers about justification even if he offered no right ones; he simply concentrated on deepening his readers' relationship to God.[11]

The Reformation: The Flowering of the Evangelical Impulse

No one who has read extensively in Luther and Calvin can doubt that apart from later Puritan authors like John Owen and Jonathan Edwards, they are unmatched in spiritual depth, intellectual vigor, and biblical fidelity. Evangelical ministerial training in theology ought to include a wide use of Reformation authors along with their modern counterparts. And this is not simply a diet for ministerial students. Many evangelical laymen today are beginning to turn away from shallow anecdotal books to look for meat rather than milk and spiritual junk food. Republications of Puritan authors have sold in the hundreds of thousands in the past decade; there is no doubt that a carefully chosen series of Luther's works would fare equally well.[12]

There has been a great resurgence of interest among younger evangelicals recently in the Radical Reformation. The uncompromising prophetic stance and the ethical consistency of men like Balthasar Hubmeier and Menno Simons needs to be appreciated by "establishment evangelicals" today. The whole church should read these writers and the new efflorescence of secondary literature about them.[13] To avoid repeating the tragic conflict between the magisterial Reformers and their Anabaptist critics, which is being replayed today not as farce but as tragedy, younger "radical Christians" should also read Luther and Calvin in order to understand the vital core of doctrine that has remained the center of the evangelical heritage. There is no reason for us to choose either the values represented by the Reformers or those of the Radical Reformation.

The same can perhaps be said about the evangelical use of the products of the Catholic Counter-Reformation: Here is another fence that needs mending. At first glance it is inconceivable that the grace and power of the Holy Spirit could be at work simultaneously in the monastic reformer Teresa of Avila and in the Protestant Reformer Martin Luther while these two were praying for one another's destruction. Nevertheless, Christians who read both are bound to conclude that this was the case, although the Spirit's work in each took different and complementary forms. Protestants who have had an excessively narrow vision of the broad arena in which the Holy Spirit has worked since the Reformation have isolated themselves from a great treasury of spiritual wisdom and artistry. They have cut themselves off from persons and works of great genius: Teresa, John of the Cross, Francis de Sales, Gerard Manley Hopkins, Graham Greene, Flannery O'Connor, Thomas Merton, and many others. Perhaps the generation of

today, which has embraced with equal delight C. S. Lewis and
J.R.R. Tolkien, is not likely to follow their predecessors in this
error.[14]

Puritanism and Pietism: Protestant Live Orthodoxy

In the second and third generations after the Reformation,
Protestant leaders found that the reform of the church was a
much more complex matter than simply designing new confessional statements and structures of polity. Even Luther had
recognized that his German constituency behaved more like a
pre-Christian "people movement" than a reformed church,
and he had suggested in 1527 that small renewal groups of
thoroughly converted Christians could function as spiritual
leaven to transform the inert larger population.[15] Luther
seems not to have followed out this strategy of renewal, but the
effort to renew the church's ministry and laity was picked up
again by the Lutheran Pietists, and by Puritan Calvinists in
England who were nonseparatists. The majority of the Pietists
and Puritans were united in insisting that ministers and church
members should reform not only their doctrines but their
lives. Their leaders during the seventeenth century worked to
create theologies of "live orthodoxy" that challenged individuals and congregations to move beyond mere "notional" mental
commitment and belief to conversion, personal faith in Christ,
and spiritual renewal. Like the Anabaptists, the Puritans and
Pietists emphasized regeneration, the process of being "born
again."

These twin movements of live orthodoxy, Pietism and
Puritanism, are undoubtedly the next stage in the outworking
of the evangelical impulse after the Reformation, adding a
balancing stress on sanctification to the Reformers' great discovery, justification by faith. Puritan and Pietist leaders wrote
some of the richest theological literature in their respective
traditions, intellectually acute and also spiritually profound.
They dealt with the work of the Holy Spirit and the Christian
life with a breadth and thoroughness that is remarkably edify-
ing, in spite of the occasional tinge of legalism remaining in

their reformulation of patristic and medieval spirituality on a Reformation base. The Puritans are the church fathers of English and American Christianity and should be read with respectful awareness that God speaks with particular clarity to the spiritual founders of a national tradition. Today the republished writings of John Owen, Richard Sibbes, Thomas Goodwin, Thomas Manton, and other Puritan authors are joining the works of John Bunyan and Richard Baxter in achieving general recognition among Protestants. A great deal of translation and republication still remains to be done before the devotional and theological classics of Johann Arndt, Philipp Spener, and August Herrmann Francke are available to American readers. Catholic Christians who are interested in evangelical Protestant spirituality cannot do better than begin by reading the Puritans and Pietists.[16]

Movements of Evangelical Awakening

The next stage in the unfolding of the evangelical impulse arose directly out of the movements of Protestant live orthodoxy, in the wave of evangelical renewal called the Great Awakening, which began around 1727 and worked through Moravian Pietism, Wesleyanism, Arminianism, and American Calvinism. All of these awakening movements made use of live orthodox theologies already forged, but added a new stress on prayerful expectation of Pentecostal outpourings of the Holy Spirit to quicken the growth of the languishing Protestant movement and a new effort at ecumenical union and cooperation among the denominational fragments which had broken apart during the seventeenth century.

If we search for the prototype of the present evangelical movement, which exists as an international, pandenominational renewal movement of Protestant live orthodoxy operating in an informal ecumenical union, we only have to go back to the alliance that emerged from the Great Awakening. This evangelical alliance, in which common goals and shared spiritual vitality led to the transcendence of confessional barriers among Lutherans and Calvinists and Arminians, inaugurated powerful movements of home and foreign missions that included both the proclamation and the social demonstration of the gospel. Evangelical missions and social reform continued at an even greater pace in the Second Awakening during the first half of the nineteenth century.[17]

Present-day evangelicals cannot understand the genius of the movement they have inherited if they fail to know the works of the men who led these movements. Count Zinzendorf, in the prophetic work of his community, Herrnhut, left one of the most remarkable models of Christian fellowship the church has ever seen. It was achieved on three levels: the local congregation, the prayer-support groups of which this was composed, and the interdenominational network to which the congregation was connected by prayer and communication. Zinzendorf's concept of tropes, the theory that the diversity of Christian groups was due to the fulfilment of a variety of social, cultural, and psychological needs, offered a model of mutual understanding that is still relevant. His attempts to promote communication and cooperation among denominations foreshadowed Evangelical Alliance in the nineteenth century, twentieth century evangelicalism, and even the Ecumenical Movement.[18]

John Wesley developed Whitefield's innovation of field preaching into a new thrust of outreach beyond the church, and in his writings left a deposit of theology carefully grounded in the Scriptures and important extrabiblical sources. Modern Arminians and Calvinists would experience less difficulty with one another if they would read Wesley, and it is hard to calculate the effect such reading might have on Methodism as a whole.

Jonathan Edwards's works offer a climactic synthesis of Puritan theology and spirituality and move beyond this to lay the foundations for Protestant theologies of church renewal. It is likely that no vital evangelical theology can emerge in America that does not make contact with Edwards's thinking.[19]

It is equally important that evangelicals study the unique combination of renewal, nurture, evangelism, and social reform that the leaders of the Second Awakening developed: Timothy Dwight, Lyman Beecher, and Charles Finney in America; and John Newton, William Wilberforce, Charles Simeon, and Lord Shaftesbury in England. The responsibility for justice and the shaping of society and culture these men assumed is a virtue that modern evangelicalism is morally bound to recover.[20]

We must recognize some continued expressions of the evangelical impulse in church reform and devotional life within the Roman Catholic and Eastern Orthodox churches in the centuries after the Reformation. The Pauline and Augustinian piety of the school of Berulle and Condren, and Faber's *All for Jesus* are thoroughly evangelical in expression, and probably had some influence on Protestant spirituality.[21]

However, the main *theological* continuation of the evangelical impulse in the church during the eighteenth and nineteenth centuries is contained within the streams involved in the First and Second Awakenings. In the course of the nineteenth century, however, the American evangelical stream began to suffer constriction and reduction. This did not occur without further development and some positive gains: Charles Finney and D. L. Moody, whose native intuitions were never disturbed by seminary education, popularized the gospel in a way that brought the laity into the process of witness as never before.

But there were losses in this process also. The frontline work of evangelical renewal was no longer led by men with the intellectual and theological stature of Edwards and Wesley, but by practical tacticians and engineers promoting the gospel with a heavy admixture of human persuasion, although the role of the Holy Spirit was still theoretically acknowledged. Revival became revivalism; what had been a comprehensive program of church renewal, evangelism, and social and cultural reform, became increasingly limited to one expression of mission: mass evangelism and personal outreach through the local church. By the 1830s, denominations and confessional theologians were beginning to react against the new revivalism, and the intellectual leadership began to move away from the Puritan goal of live orthodoxy toward a cooler systematic expression of the faith, under increasing pressure from explosions of secular thought in the surrounding culture that were pushing some Protestants into heterodoxy.[22]

The Division of the Evangelical Stream

By the end of the nineteenth century, the stream of American evangelical Protestantism was beginning to fan out and break up into smaller, shallower rivulets like a river delta.

One main stream of leaders carried the concerns for evangelism, spiritual growth, and orthodox theology into fundamentalism, Pentecostalism, and several related streamlets of confessional orthodoxy. A second main branch carried the original evangelical concern for social reform into a new channel, the Social Gospel, paralleling another new rivulet of liberal theology, retaining also the concern for ecumenical unity among denominations that characterized the awakening tradition. It is tempting for modern evangelicals to regard this "Delta Effect" as a division between light and darkness, Christ and Antichrist. But the fact is that the "Christocentric Liberals" were often the children of fundamentalists reacting against theological and cultural shallowness in that movement, and they frequently retained a real if vaguely expressed allegiance to Jesus Christ as Lord and Savior.

By the 1930s another stream had appeared in the delta, neo-orthodoxy, reacting both against liberalism and fundamentalism and seeking to mediate between them. Despite the weaknesses in this movement, part of it expressed some of the intellectual rigor and biblical insight characteristic of the original evangelical impulse.

Meanwhile a comparable intellectual and theological stream was developing adjacent to fundamentalism, springing from Abraham Kuyper, B. B. Warfield, and J. Gresham Machen. It was out of this stream and fundamentalist revivalism that a new reform movement appeared in the 1940s seeking to recover the original force of the evangelical tradition. It is this interdenominational and international movement of purified fundamentalist revivalism, in coalition with several forms of confessional orthodoxy, which we call evangelicalism.[23]

The Recovery of Evangelical Catholicity

In the disorderly but genuine process of renewal taking place in the church today, there is a real convergence between some of the streams in the delta, as Christians seek to recover the evangelical synthesis that was broken into diverging movements at the beginning of this century. Neo-orthodox churchmen are recognizing the spiritual vitality and fertility of evangelicals, and younger evangelicals are recognizing that the social awareness and compassion they encounter in Christians on the left is often a deaconal instinct that is part of the evangelical impulse and a genuine gift of the Spirit. If the complementary weaknesses of "liberal" and "conservative" Protestants are ever to be healed, if the shattered genetic pool of classical evangelicalism is ever to be recovered and reassembled, there must be sharing and dialog between some of the opposing parties in contemporary Protestantism, along with a recovery of the Catholic heritage of the past.

At this point it may seem to the reader that in our effort to avoid "a reduction of the historic faith" we have been too inclusive and indiscriminate, that we have recognized as genuine parts of Christ's body, and real expressions of the evangelical impulse, movements and doctrinal structures that are really antithetical to one another. There is certainly a real danger of trying to embrace both light and darkness and to bring peace where Christ would bring a sword. We dare not move beyond the biblical limits of the gospel. We should be aware that classical evangelicalism always ran a double risk of veering off either to the left or the right, leaving the difficult task of cleaving together in a consensus of live orthodoxy, and wandering off into pious heresy, or splitting up into a handful of dead and contentious confessional orthodoxies. The indiscriminate piety that holds that "doctrine divides, but Jesus unites" is just as dangerous to the church's health as the cold

Pharisaism that dismembers the body of Christ by its legal rigor.

Suppose we acknowledge that the evangelical impulse is behind some of the strivings toward renewal in the Catholic Pentecostal movement; this does not mean that there are not hard and serious doctrinal problems to be solved before Protestants can silence their prophetic challenge to their Catholic brothers and sisters. Suppose that we detect the Spirit of Christ at work among the many winds of doctrine that sweep through nonevangelical Protestantism; this does not mean that we should weld truth to falsehood, or compromise the integrity and clarity of our systematic understanding of the gospel by saying that doctrinal precision does not matter. What it does mean is that we should cleave to these brethren with love, prayer, and communication, until the body of Christ achieves the goal of unity that Spener and Edwards predicted once the parts had been revived. Classical evangelicals welcomed denominational pluralism in dialog, but they always fought the kind of insulary pluralism in which Christians ignore one another or shout past one another in self-righteous anger.[24]

Evangelicals worry that Catholic ecumenicism is the threat of an ocean to swallow a pond, and they do not even feel easy about digging trenches between themselves and other ponds. Denominationally, however, there are no oceans, only lakes, and the life in these is joined in an ecosystem that cannot flourish while they are separate. There is often a necessity to draw apart from one another in certain dimensions in order to preserve the integrity of our witness and sometimes our life itself. However, there is visible in history what might be called *the principle of catholicity: Whenever genuine parts of Christ's body write one another off as demonic, lose all respect for one another, and move apart so far that they lose all mechanisms for communication and dialog, they rob themselves of the full treasure of the Christian heritage, and inevitably move in polar directions into darkness, weakness, and ultimately into heresy.* The biblical basis for this is Paul's great prophecy for the church's future, which states that we are bound to be ". . . children, tossed here and there by waves, and carried about by every wind of doctrine . . ." until ". . . speaking the truth in love, we . . . grow up . . . into Him, who is the head . . . from . . . which every joint supplies, according to the proper working of each individual part, causes the growth of the body for the building up of itself in love." (Eph. 4:14–16, NASB).

The catholic principle is simply Zinzendorf's ecumenical principle applied consistently throughout history. Unless modern evangelicals adopt this principle, they will remain alienated from the spirit of classical evangelicalism, and will inevitably suffer a reduction of the historic faith.

Notes

1. For a review of social and cultural transformations emerging from evangelical Christianity during past periods of awakening, and a program for the extension and deepening of the present awakening, see my *Dynamics of Spiritual Life: an Evangelical Theology of Renewal,* to be published soon by InterVarsity Press.

2. Philip Schaff, *The Principle of Protestantism,* trans. John W. Nevin (Philadelphia: United Church Press, 1964).

3. Thomas F. Torrance, *The Doctrine of Grace in the Apostolic Fathers* (Grand Rapids: Eerdmans, 1959).

4. Martin Luther, *Works,* ed. Jaroslav Pelikan, vol. 54 (Philadelphia: Fortress Press, 1965), p. 340.

5. Perhaps the best introduction to the body of sources mentioned in this paragraph is J. Stevenson's collection, *A New Eusebius* (London: S.P.C.K., 1957).

6. An exploration of Augustine should probably begin with the *Confessions, On the Letter and the Spirit,* and *The City of God,* and then move on to embrace the other works contained in *Basic Writings of Saint Augustine,* ed. Whitney J. Oates (New York: Random House, 1948). Two secondary studies that will prove helpful are Roy Battenhouse's *Companion to the Study of St. Augustine* (New York: Oxford Univ. Press, 1955), and Peter Brown's *Augustine of Hippo: A Biography* (Berkeley: Univ. of California Press, 1967).

7. Those interested in a simple introduction to the theology of the councils should consult J.W.C. Wand's *The Four Great Heresies* (London: A.R. Mowbray & Co., 1955) and should also examine Philip

Schaff's *The Creeds of Christendom* (New York: Harper and Bros., 1877).

8. The simplest and richest introduction to the ascetic tradition is still H.B. Workman's *Persecution in the Early Church* (London: Charles H. Kelly, 1906). The reader should also examine the *Benedictine Rule*, which can be found in *Western Asceticism*, ed. Owen Chadwick (Philadelphia: Westminster Press, 1958).

9. Cf. Josef Pieper, *Scholasticism*, trans. Richard and Clara Winston (London: Faber and Faber, 1960).

10. Those looking for an introduction to this literature should read Bernard of Clairvaux, *The Twelve Degrees of Humility and Pride*, trans. B.R.V. Mills (New York: Macmillan and Co., 1929); *St. Bernard of Clairvaux Seen Through His Selected Letters*, trans. Bruno Scott James (Chicago: H. Regnery Co., 1953); and Bonaventure's *The Mind's Road to God*, trans. George Boas, Jr. (New York: Bobbs-Merrill Co., 1953). See also P. Pourrat's *Christian Spirituality*, trans. W.H. Mitchell and S.P. Jacques, vol. 2 (Westminster, Md.: Newman Press, 1953), which provides an overview of medieval piety that is more accessible to the average reader than Louis Bouyer's careful and scholarly *History of Christian Spirituality* (London: Burns and Oates, 1963–1968).

11. A minimal knowledge of this literature should probably include John Tauler's *Signposts to Perfection*, ed. and trans. Elizabeth Strakosch (St. Louis: Herder, 1958); Thomas à Kempis's *The Imitation of Christ*, trans. Ronald Knox and Michael Oakley (New York: Sheed and Ward, 1960), and Brother Lawrence's *The Practice of the Presence of God.*

12. Along with Roland Bainton's *Here I Stand* (New York: Abingdon-Cokesbury Press, 1950), the layman investigating Luther should read the *Commentary on Galatians* (1536), ed. Jaroslav Pelikan, vols. 26 and 27 (Philadelphia: Fortress Press, 1963), and the central reformational treatises contained in volumes 31–34 of the Pelikan edition of Luther's works. The *Institutes of the Christian Religion* is the best introduction to the mind of Calvin, along with John T. McNeill's *The History and Character of Calvinism* (New York: Oxford Univ. Press, 1954).

13. A clear and simple introduction to the Radical Reformation is William Estep's *The Anabaptist Story* (Grand Rapids: Eerdmans, 1963). Also helpful is Roland Bainton's *The Travail of Religious Liberty* (New York: Harper and Bros., 1958). We still have a great need for Anabaptist sources in English translation, but the following will be helpful: *Spiritual and Anabaptist Writers*, ed. George H. Williams and A.M. Mergal (Philadelphia: Westminster Press, 1957), and *The Complete Writings of Menno Simons*, trans. Leonard Verduin (Scottsdale, Pa.: Mennonite Publishing House, 1956).

14. I would recommend Alexander Whyte's *Santa Teresa: an Appreciation* (New York: Fleming H. Revell, 1898) as a good introduction for Protestants, along with Teresa's autobiography (in *The Complete Works . . .* , trans and ed. E. Allison Peers [London: Sheed and Ward, 1946]); *The Dark Night of the Soul*, by John of the Cross (in *The Complete Works*, trans. and ed. E. Allison Peers [Westminster, Md.: The Newman Press, 1964]); and the *Introduction to the Devout Life* of Francis de Sales, trans. and ed. John K. Ryan (New York: Harper and Bros., 1952).

15. Martin Luther, "Preface" to *The German Mass*, in Luther's *Works*, ed. Jaroslav Pelikan, vol. 53 (Philadelphia: Fortress Press, 1965).

16. Evangelical readers can obtain a good introduction to this literature in Gordon Wakefield's *Puritan Devotion* (London: Epworth Press, 1957); Donald Bloesch, *The Evangelical Renaissance* (Grand Rapids: Eerdmans, 1973); and F.E. Stoeffler, *The Rise of Evangelical Pietism* (Leiden: Brill and Co., 1965) and *German Pietism in the Eighteenth Century* (Leiden: Brill and Co., 1973). Basic sources that the average reader will find helpful are John Owen's *Temptation and Sin* (Grand Rapids: Zondervan, 1958) and *The Glory of Christ* (Chicago: Moody Press, 1949); Richard Sibbes's *The Bruised Reed and Smoking Flax* in *Puritan Works of Richard Sibbes*, ed. A.B. Grosart (London: Banner of Truth Trust, 1973); Thomas Goodwin's *A Child of Light Walking in Darkness,* in *Works*, vol. 3 (Edinburgh: James Nichol, 1861); Bunyan's *Pilgrim's Progress, The Holy War,* and *Grace Abounding to the Chief of Sinners;* William Gurnall's *The Christian in Complete Armor* (Evansville, Ind.: Sovereign Grace Book Club, 1958); Richard Baxter's *The Reformed Pastor,* ed. Hugh Martin (London: SCM Press, 1956), and *The Saints' Everlasting Rest,* abridged with an introduction by John T. Wilkinson (London: Epworth Press, 1962). Basic Pietist sources include Johann Arndt's *True Christianity* (London, n.p., 1710), which obviously needs a new translation, and Philipp Jakob Spener's *Pia Desideria,* trans. and ed. Theodore G. Tappert (Philadelphia: Fortress Press, 1964).

17. The roots of the evangelical movement in the late seventeenth- and eighteenth-century awakening periods are described in my *Dynamics of Spiritual Life: an Evangelical Theology of Renewal* and *The American Pietism of Cotton Mather: Origins of American Evangelicalism,* both shortly to be published; and in Arthur Skevington Wood's *The Inextinguishable Blaze* (London: Paternoster Press, 1960).

18. A simple but effective and fascinating introduction to the genius of Zinzendorf is A.J. Lewis's *Zinzendorf the Ecumenical Pioneer* (Philadelphia: Westminster Press, 1962).

19. Wesley is best encountered in his *Journal,* abridged by

Nehemiah Curnock (London: Epworth Press, 1958), and his *Standard Sermons,* ed. Edward H. Sugden (London: Epworth Press, 1961). Edwards's major writings on the theology of spiritual renewal are probably the best introduction to his mind; see *The Great Awakening,* ed. C.C. Goen (New Haven: Yale Univ. Press, 1972); *The Religious Affections,* ed. John E. Smith (New Haven: Yale Univ. Press, 1959); and such sermons as *A Divine and Supernatural Light* and *The Excellency of Christ.*

20. Lyman Beecher's *Autobiography,* ed. Barbara M. Cross (Cambridge: Harvard Univ. Press, 1961), and Charles Finney's *Lectures on Revivals of Religion,* ed. William G. McLoughlin (Cambridge: Harvard Univ. Press, 1960), are good reflections of the American phase of the Second Awakening. William Wilberforce's *Practical View of The Prevailing Religious System of Professed Christians* (Boston: Nathaniel Willis, 1815) affords a complementary view of the English phase. Secondary studies on the Second Awakening include J. Edwin Orr's *The Light of Nations* (Grand Rapids: Eerdmans, 1965), George Marsden's *The Evangelical Mind and the New School Presbyterian Experience* (New Haven: Yale Univ. Press, 1970), and E.M. Howse's *Saints in Politics* (London: Allen, 1953).

21. For a survey of this material see P. Pourrat, *History of Christian Spirituality,* Vol. IV.

22. The gains and losses during this period can be assessed on the one hand by examining J. Edwin Orr's *The Second Evangelical Awakening in America* (London: Marshall, 1952), and on the other hand by William McLoughlin's *Modern Revivalism* (New York: Ronald Press Co., 1959). We are still awaiting a sharp and concise account of the degeneration and division of theological streams at the turn of the century. For elaboration of "the Delta Effect," see "The Spiritual Roots of Christian Social Reform" in my *Dynamics of Spiritual Life.*

23. A concise account of the development of American evangelicalism in the twentieth century is available in Richard Quebedeaux's *The Young Evangelicals* (New York: Harper and Row, 1974). Carl Henry's *The Uneasy Conscience of Modern Fundamentalism* (Grand Rapids: Eerdmans, 1947) and *The Case for Orthodox Theology* (Philadelphia: Westminster, 1959) are helpful source documents illuminating this reform movement.

24. Some theological structures, such as the old liberalism described in J. Gresham Machen's *Christianity and Liberalism* (New York: Macmillan Co., 1923) and the theology of Paul Tillich, appear to be alternate gospels, although they may contain instructive insights and be held by persons who are severely confused but regenerate believers. Other theologies that may not be consistently evangelical, and

may contain very serious weaknesses, seem to issue nonetheless from a powerful evangelical impulse (e.g., the work of P.T. Forsyth, Karl Barth, Emil Brunner, Dietrich Bonhoeffer, the Niebuhrs, and Helmut Thielicke). Our greatest danger with respect to such men and their followers is probably not so much the dilution of our own orthodoxy through dialog and fellowship, but the loss through our estrangement of their valid biblical insights and the potential of their further movement in an evangelical direction. For further reflection on this see "Live Orthodoxy" and "Unitive Evangelicalism" in *Dynamics of Spiritual Life*. For a constructive appreciation and critique of nonevangelical theologians, see Philip Edgecumbe Hughes, ed., *Creative Minds in Contemporary Theology* (Grand Rapids: Eerdmans, 1969).

4. A Call to Biblical Fidelity
by

ROGER NICOLE

Roger Nicole is Professor of Systematic Theology at Gordon-Conwell Theological Seminary in South Hamilton, Massachusetts. He holds the Ph.D. from Harvard University. He is the author of many articles and coauthor of A Bibliography of Benjamin Breckinridge Warfield

We deplore our tendency toward individualistic interpretation of Scripture. This undercuts the objective character of biblical truth, and denies the guidance of the Holy Spirit among his people through the ages.

Therefore we affirm that the Bible is to be interpreted in keeping with the best insights of historical and literary study, under the guidance of the Holy Spirit, with respect for the historic understanding of the church.

We affirm that the Scriptures, as the infallible Word of God, are the basis of authority in the church. We acknowledge that God uses the Scriptures to judge and to purify his Body. The church, illumined and guided by the Holy Spirit, must in every age interpret, proclaim and live out the Scriptures.

Evangelicals have always and everywhere recognized the supreme authority of the Bible. They do not claim to be the only ones who have ever done so, but they do contend that a wholehearted commitment to the supreme authority of Scripture is an indispensable constituent of the evangelical profession. This kind of affirmation could easily be documented in the writings of countless representative leaders of the evangelical movement, and also in the confessions of faith that have served as a rallying point for evangelical individuals and institutions.[1]

In making this profession, evangelicals gratefully acknowledge that their view is not an isolated outpost in the history of the church of Christ, but that a recognition of the authority of God speaking in His written Word has been a common characteristic of much of the stream of historic Christianity. Notably, at the time of the Reformation of the sixteenth century, the call to the authority of Scripture was a fundamental uniting feature of the orthodox Reformation.[2]

Further back in time than the Reformation, modern evangelicals have also found a kindred spirit in the attitude toward the Scripture of many of the Fathers of the church. In fact a pivotal part of the evangelical approach is based on the claim that the recognition of the supreme authority of the Bible is steeped in the attitude of our Lord Himself and of the apostles toward the Old Testament Scripture. The evangelical therefore observes a continuum between the attitude of orthodox and pious Jews of the old covenant, the stance of our Lord and the apostles, the view of the early church and of many of the key leaders in the church to the time of the Reformation, the outlook of the Reformers themselves and of their most notable successors, and the witness of those who are accounted leaders in the evangelical movement since the seventeenth century. Here we have therefore not a provincial and obscurantist outlook, but rather a great consensus to which once again attention must be called.

It has been the desire of those who participated in the Chicago Call conference to assert this with unmistakable clarity and in such a breadth of understanding as not to precipitate internal divisive quarrels concerning certain specifications in this common confession, but to emphasize in a positive manner our wholehearted commitment to the authority of the Scripture, viewed as the Word of God.

To make this commitment has some weighty implications in a number of practical issues. We limit our presentation here to three important ones.

I. The Text of Scripture

Because the Bible is the Word of God, it is particularly important for us to establish as closely as we can the precise text as it was written in its original production. Textual criticism, which is a matter of interest for historical and literary purposes in connection with other writings, becomes a matter of paramount significance for those who sense that in the Bible we have the very words that God intended to serve as the norm for His church.

Some evangelicals in a rather obscurantist manner have at times viewed textual criticism with suspicion, as if it were the tool of a dangerous enemy bent upon manipulating the Scripture in order to suit some views that were alien to what God had established. It is precisely the reverse that is true: Textual criticism is a strong ally in the acceptance of the divine authority of Scripture, and it is its supreme purpose to recover with a maximum of accuracy the precise form in which the oracles of God were at first couched. An enlightened evangelical will therefore be grateful for every discovery that enables us to ascertain with greater accuracy what the autographic text has been.

Meanwhile, the evangelical will also gladly acknowledge that even in the manuscripts or translations of Scripture in which some deviations have occurred there remains such a high degree of integrity that they can function, and have effectually functioned, as appropriate representatives of the divine authority vested in Scripture. It is a remarkable thing that some people who do not hold a particularly high view of the divine inspiration of Scripture have nevertheless devoted hours of scholarly research to the task of establishing the text. It is a matter of regret that some evangelicals, who ought to have a maximum interest in securing the right text, have at times been contemptuous of the efforts and methods by which this can best be accomplished.[3]

II. The Translations

If the Bible is indeed the Word of God, it is of crucial significance that its message be transmitted in as many languages as possible with a maximum degree of accuracy. Evangelicals therefore have rightly been in the forefront of the establishment of biblical societies that have made it their business to provide the text of Scripture on a wide scale. They have also promoted the translation of the Scripture into many languages, and the Wycliffe Bible Translators are particularly noteworthy in recent years for their endeavors in this respect.

Here again, however, there has been at times an unfortunate tendency to "canonize" particular translations. One can easily understand the attachment of some people to the stately forms and beautiful cadences of the King James translation. But the facts remain that this version was based on a text that is viewed by many as imperfect in a number of details, and that it is couched in a form of English so obsolete as to represent a serious barrier to understanding for the average English-speaking person in our day. There is therefore a continuing need to update and to present the Bible in the language of the people. This needs to be done with dignity but without a pedantic attachment to literary forms that have become obsolete. It may be permissible at this point to mention the considerable effort made in producing modern translations of the Bible in the vernacular, and particularly the joint effort of many evangelical scholars in the production of the *New International Version,* to single out only one recent translation in English.

What a translation needs is to say everything that the text said and no more, while retaining something of the scope and the lively characteristics found in the original. It is very difficult to achieve this for any text. Therefore, one who is not acquainted with the original languages will do well to compare translations in order to distinguish between what is original Scripture and what has been added in the translating process in order to be sure that he has not lost anything of what God said through the original text. Commentaries help us in this process, but nothing can really replace the close personal study of the Bible itself.

III. Interpretation

It is essential that the Bible be understood to say what it means, and in order to achieve this purpose, it is necessary to observe two safeguards:

Contextual Interpretation

One needs to take account very carefully of the context in which any statement is found. The very first task of the interpreter is to ascertain what a passage or statement meant to the people to whom it was at first addressed. This is the first principle of historico-grammatical exegesis, and it has been since the Reformation a major element in the evangelical outlook. We do not need to deny wholly the propriety of what is called the *sensus plenior,* but we need to recognize the primacy of the original meaning seen in its historical perspective. One reason why the commentaries of Calvin are still notably useful in our day is that he adhered so strenuously to this principle. By contrast others who have indulged in allegorizing interpretations are generally thought to be less effective exponents of Scripture. As evangelicals we need to be ever reminded that the supreme authority of Scripture will best be safeguarded when the Scripture has the freedom to say exactly what it said, and when its mandates are not forced into patterns of thinking that we cherish but which may very well not have a divine warrant.

Interpretation within the Communion of the Saints

In the interpreting process it is very important to avoid the *Scylla* of undue attachment to tradition and the *Charybdis* of vagrant individual arbitrariness.

Surely the fact that we are living in the twentieth century demands that we should acknowledge the value of accumulated labors spent upon the Scriptures. We are not confronted by the task of interpreting as if God had never worked heretofore among His people. Rather, the Bible was born in the midst of God's people of the old and the new covenants. It bears the stamp of their own circumstances and understanding, and it is received by individuals through the mediacy of the church. This consideration, however, did in the past lead to some serious distortions, to the extent that on some occasions the Bible seemed to become the captive of human tradition. This had already occurred among the Jews, and Christ castigated severely the Pharisees and the teachers of the Law with the charge: "You nullify the word of God by your tradition that you have handed down . . ." (Mark 7:13, NIV).

At the time of the Reformation a situation that appears analogous in many respects prevailed, and one of the concerns of the Reformers was to bring back the focus of attention upon the Scripture in its original form so that the church would be delivered from accretions and distortions that threatened the integrity of divine authority. This lesson, learned through such harrowing conflicts, ought never to be forgotten. The Bible must have a place in which it has opportunity to speak directly to people without the interposition of a human screen that might tamper with the biblical message.

To speak in this manner, however, does not mean that the door must be left open for any kind of vagaries developed by individual imagination on the pretense that one is interpreting the Bible. Here again the pages of church history are burdened with solemn warnings about the gravity of fanciful or disorderly private interpretations. It is important to recognize that a sober understanding of the Scripture must take place in the midst of the community of faith. The best commentaries are usually steeped in the whole history of the interpretation of the text. Those who would disconnect themselves from the labors of the past are impoverishing their own outlook by cutting off meaningful roots that could give them stability and perspective in understanding the Word of God. They are paying an insult to the work of the Holy Spirit by assuming that His agency in the midst of God's people for nearly two thousand years is so inconsequential that it can be glibly disregarded without detriment to our understanding of the Scripture.

It isn't easy to steer a clear course between these twin shoals. Some who are especially burdened to maintain the significance of corporate understanding may be subtly led into the temptation of subordinating the Scripture to tradition. Others who are especially eager to safeguard their right to approach the Bible directly may in the process be led into the temptation of absolutizing their own judgment—yes, even their vagaries. In the Chicago Call conference a studied concern was expressed that evangelicals should be especially careful to avoid the latter danger, since this was the temptation into which they are more likely to fall.

That we may steer a proper course may, however, be expected, hopefully without a rash presumption, because of the great comfort of the doctrine of the *perspicuity of Scripture*. In the matters in which God desires to instruct us, His Word is clear, and if we observe the safeguards which He has provided for us in the communication of the whole Bible rather than just parts of it, and in the enlightenment of His Spirit as given to His people through the ages, we may feel confident that we shall be led into the truth in the areas where this matters supremely for our spiritual life and welfare. It is with this confidence at heart that evangelicals must call the whole church, including themselves, to an ever-renewed commitment to biblical fidelity.

Notes

1. The following statements may be considered as representative both of the range of views expressed in such confessions of faith and of the range of organizations that accept such a banner.

"The divine inspiration, authority, and sufficiency of the holy Scriptures." *Evangelical Alliance,* 1846.

"We believe the Bible to be the inspired, the only infallible, authoritative word of God." *National Association of Evangelicals,* 1942.

"We believe in the holy Scripture as originally given by God, divinely inspired, infallible, entirely trustworthy, and the supreme authority in all matters of faith and conduct." *World Evangelical Fellowship,* 1947.

"The Bible alone and the Bible in its entirety is the word of God written, and therefore inerrant in the autographs." *Evangelical Theological Society,* 1949.

"The unique, divine inspiration, entire trustworthiness and authority of the Bible," *Inter-Varsity Christian Fellowship.*

"We believe that the Bible, consisting of the Old and New Testaments only, is verbally inspired by the Holy Spirit, is inerrant in the original manuscripts, and is the infallible and authoritative Word of God," *Interdenominational Foreign Mission Association.*

"We affirm the divine inspiration, truthfulness and authority of both Old and New Testament Scriptures in their entirety as the only written Word of God, without error in all that it affirms, and the only infallible rule of faith and practice. We also affirm the power of God's Word to accomplish his purpose of salvation. The message of the Bible is addressed to all mankind. For God's revelation in Christ and in Scripture is unchangeable. Through it the Holy Spirit still speaks today. He illumines the minds of God's people in every culture to perceive its truth freshly through their own eyes and thus discloses to the whole church ever more of the many-colored wisdom of God." *Lousanne Covenant,* 1974.

2. The so-called "left-wing" or Radical Reformation sometimes manifested the tendency to discard the authority of Scripture or to supplant it by an appeal to the rational powers of man or to some inner light given to individuals. But precisely at this point the mainline Reformers were united in rejecting these approaches as *Schwärmerei* and in committing themselves resolutely to the acceptance of the

written Word as the norm by which anything else that claimed to have a divine mandate had to be judged or regulated.

3. It is worthwhile to note here that B.B. Warfield, who is well-known for his strong advocacy of a "high" view of inspiration, was also a leading exponent of modern and effective methods for the textual criticism of the New Testament. One of his earliest published works was *An Introduction to the Textual Criticism of the New Testament* (London: Hodder and Stoughton, 1886).

5. A Call to Creedal Identity
by

MORRIS INCH

Morris Inch is Professor of Theology and Chair-
man of the Biblical Studies Department at
Wheaton College, Wheaton, Illinois. He earned
the Ph.D. at Boston University and is the author
of a number of books including Understanding
Biblical Prophecy *(New York: Harper & Row,*
1977), and The Evangelical Challenge
(Philadelphia: Westminster Press, 1978).

We deplore two opposite excesses: a creedal church that merely recites a
faith inherited from the past, and a creedless church that languishes in
a doctrinal vacuum. We confess that as evangelicals we are not
immune from these defects.

Therefore we affirm the need in our time for a confessing
church that will boldly witness to its faith before the world, even
under threat of persecution. In every age the church must state its
faith over against heresy and paganism. What is needed is a
vibrant confession that excludes as well as includes, and thereby
aims to purify faith and practice. Confessional authority is limited
by and derived from the authority of Scripture, which alone

remains ultimately and permanently normative. Nevertheless, as the common insight of those who have been illumined by the Holy Spirit and seek to be the voice of the "holy catholic church," a confession should serve as a guide for the interpretation of Scripture.

We affirm the abiding value of the great ecumenical creeds and the Reformation confessions. Since such statements are historically and culturally conditioned, however, the church today needs to express its faith afresh, without defecting from the truths apprehended in the past. We need to articulate our witness against the idolatries and false ideologies of our day.

Christian faith is creedal. It seeks to express its convictions, both individually (as testimonial) and corporately (in creed or confession). We shall concern ourselves with the latter feature, the corporate expression of Christian faith.

Alternatives

The Chicago Call identifies two extremes: "a creedal church that merely recites a faith inherited from the past, and a creedless church that languishes in a doctrinal vacuum." There is wisdom in recognizing these opposite dangers. C. S. Lewis reminds us that the devil "always sends errors into the world in pairs—pairs of opposites. And he always encourages us to spend a lot of time thinking which is the worse. You see why, of course? He relies on your extra dislike of the one error to draw you gradually into the opposite one."[1]

We may err as easily in one direction as the other—in meaningless recitation of the creeds or a languishing creedlessness. Some shudder at the thought of Christians expressing themselves differently and retreat into an uncritical affirmation of the creeds; others complain that the creeds infringe on Christian liberty in order to justify their peculiar theological preference. Both views alike court disaster.

Vain repetitions of the creed, of course, will not suffice. Arthur Cochrane points out that we confess "a living person who is the Lord and thus calls for a personal relationship of trust and obedience to him—not the confession as such or to the doctrines contained in it."[2] We confess to Him, in the presence of others, our trust and obedience. Anything less makes a mockery out of the creed.

But creedlessness provides no better solution. The first of the counts against creedlessness is that we are called to Christ, and not just any Christ but the Christ of Scripture. We do "not confess a mystical Christ who may be apprehended in the general religious consciousness, in world history, or in reason and experience, but the Christ whom the church hears as the witness of the Old and New Testaments."[3] We confess the Jesus who appeared to fulfill the Messianic promises of the prophets before Him, and this fact excludes a private interpretation in its strictest sense. He is the Christ of the prophets and apostles; He is not a creation of one's fancy.

Christ is what creeds are made of, but creeds are corporate confessions as well. We come to Jesus and inevitably find that there are those who have preceded us and others who will follow. There is a company of believers called out from the world to serve the Lord. This is the second reason why a creedless alternative must be denied.

Jesus reminds us of our life together. He taught us to pray "Our Father. . . Give *us* this day *our* daily bread. . . . Forgive *us* *our* debts. . . . And do not lead *us* into temptation, but deliver *us* from evil . . . " (Matt. 6:9–13, NASB, italics added). We can only confess Him as we confess together, drawing from our common faith.

Finally, we confess our faith before the world. We look around to see that vast company from which we have come, to sense that they look to us as the professed followers of Christ, and to view them as the recipients of our ministry in Christ's name. Our confession is located in time and place. It speaks of a common concern for those we serve.

What is the problem with creedlessness? It fails to appreciate that we must confess Christ in the church and before the world. It misjudges the nature of discipleship, fellowship, and service.

We reject the mere recital of the creed on the one hand and creedlessness on the other and choose to confess Christ as the church militant. Here we stand as His beachhead in a hostile world to obey His commission.

Social Dynamics

Paul instructed young Timothy: "The things which you have heard from me in the presence of many witnesses, these entrust to faithful men, who will be able to teach others also" (2 Tim. 2:2, NASB). Thus has the Christian faith been passed along from one generation to the next, each student becoming another man's instructor. And so the creed functions to impart faith, to test its reception, and to begin the cycle all over again. This is the dynamic of creedalism seen in its simplest terms.

Of course the development of any given creed is much more complicated than the previous description would lead us to believe. Erik Routley opens up the subject for us with an interesting analogy: "Looking back over the Confessions that have so far come under review, the reader cannot fail to observe in their succession a certain pattern comparable to that of a ship lurching through a heavy sea with shifting cargo. First, one, then another theological point is brought into prominence, and all the others are gathered round it."[4] We shall elaborate on this metaphor.

Routley's ship is the church. The Chicago Call reads: "In every age the church must state its faith over against heresy and paganism." *Paganism* represents that which does not presume to be the church, and *heresy* that which claims church identity and has none. The church must contend with both alike.

The term *pagan* bares some unnecessarily negative connotations. The pagan may be as religious, respectable, and cultured as his Christian counterpart. The one point at which they diverge is on the claims of Christ. The pagan does not alter his life so as to accommodate the presence of Christ; the Christian labors to hear the "well done, good and faithful servant" of his Lord.

There is a popular form of Christo-paganism abroad in the world today that may well be the most serious threat confronting the church. It fails to recognize the uncompromising nature of Christian discipleship and prostitutes the truth of God to the preferences of men.

So in our age the church is once again called upon to confront paganism with the claims of Christ. It needs to obey the Scripture's injunction to ". . . contend earnestly for the faith which was once for all delivered to the saints" (Jude 3, NASB), and one of its resources is the creed.

The creed also acts as a means for combating heresy. Thus the primary aim of those who manufactured the Nicene Creed was to overcome the Arian dissent. In fact Christian orthodoxy generally appears as a correction of one or another deviation from the truth. It sees men·being led astray and sets up a warning cry to return to the proper course.

We are reminded in the *Book of Common Prayer:* "From all false doctrine, heresy, and action, Good Lord, deliver us." Such has been the concern of the church: to chart its course away from the reefs of heresy.

The creed also provides an occasion for the church to gather itself. There are ever so many factors that differentiate Christians (language, race, nationality, vocation, interests, age, etc.), but the creed provides mutual ground. As a result we experience unity and a common allegiance that encourages purposeful diversity.

"Behold, how good and how pleasant it is For brothers to dwell together in unity!" (Ps. 133:1, NASB). The psalmist traces the gathering of God's people, through his anticipation, and to the blessing of God upon them. He continues to adorn the prospect with exceedingly rich imagery:

It is like the precious oil upon the head,
Coming down upon the beard,
Even Aaron's beard,
Coming down upon the edge of his robes.
It is like the dew of Hermon,
Coming down upon the mountain of Zion;

For there the Lord commanded the blessing—life forever
(133:2,3, NASB).

So should the church look with favor upon the creed's role in
gathering the people in anticipation of God's lavish benediction.

The creed similarly relates to the dispersal of God's people
in ministry. Arthur Cochrane warns: "A church that neglected
to draw the implications of its Confession for the social and
political order and that was concerned only about the purity of
its own teaching and piety would certainly not be a confessing
church."[5] It ought to be concerned for the purity of teaching
and piety, but not to exclude evangelism and ethics.

Lesslie Newbigin comments further: "The church is indeed
a gathering of those whom the Holy Spirit calls into the fellowship of Christ. But it is never enough for the church simply to
be there and to say 'Come.' There has to be a movement of
kenosis; one has to be willing to go, to become simply the
unrecognized servant of men where they are, in order that
there perhaps in quite new forms, the authentic substance of
the new life in Christ may take shape and become visible."[6]
Newbigin continues to liken this to a rhythm, a movement of
coming and going, gathering and scattering, where the church
realizes the purpose of Christ's calling.

The creed accompanies the church in its rhythmic movement. It signals the gathering and dispersal of the people and it
offers the blessing of God upon those who readily come and
go.

We turn our attention away from the ship (church) to its
cargo (the gospel). Paul reminds us that the essential nature of
the gospel consists of the fact ". . . that Christ died for our sins
according to the Scriptures, and that He was buried, and that
He was raised on the third day according to the Scriptures" (1
Cor. 15:3,4, NASB). The Crucifixion-Resurrection is the gospel in its most abridged form and anything that fails to incorporate this truth as its dominant feature is a false faith.

Therefore, we ought to expect a continuity with the church's cargo. We do not dispatch all the church has accepted at the port of the Enlightenment and pick up a radically different belief thereafter. The one truth sustains us throughout the total voyage.

But there is another side to this coin. We must be concerned not only with the continuity of the faith but its contemporaneity as well. The church declares the gospel to persons located in time and space and must sensitively apply that abiding message to changing situations.

Here the task seems paradoxical, for the gospel is both relevant to the situation and yet transcends the age to which it speaks. The gospel is painfully pointed, concrete, strips away hypocrisy, details responsibility, and still it never weds itself to the passing interests of the time.

We shall resist the temptation to explore this paradoxical nature of the gospel as it relates to a given time so not to be drawn afield from the subject at hand. It is enough for us to appreciate that each generation ought to hear the gospel expressed in the freshness of its own life-style and without diluting the gospel as such.

We consider as the final aspect of Routley's metaphor the heavy seas and shifting cargo. The church was never promised an easy trip. Jesus said to the disciples, " '. . . behold, I send you out as lambs in the midst of wolves' " (Luke 10:3, NASB). On another occasion, He warned: " '. . . "A slave is not greater than his master." If they persecuted Me, they will also persecute you . . .' " (John 15:20, NASB).

I have stood by the hour and felt my ship negotiate the swelling sea that would draw the bow low into the water until the craft seemed to groan in protest, and then throw it back on its stern as if to boast a greater power. So must the church strain against the rulers and powers of this world, against the forces of wickedness in high places. It charts a creedal course.

The ship's cargo often shifts more as a result of the sea swell than because of the efforts of the crew. Sometimes (generally in retrospect), the church regrets allowing the world to set its agenda. For instance, Karl Barth recalls the ready accommodation of nineteenth-century theology to its age: "Consequently it was forced to make reductions and oversimplifications, to indulge in forgetfulness and carelessness, when it dealt with the exciting and all-important matters of Christian understanding. These developments were bound to threaten, indeed to undermine, both theology and the church with impoverishment and triviality."[7]

Some theological recognition of the concerns of the time is certainly wholesome and inevitable in any case. What Barth deplored was the church's willingness to deal with pressing interests at the expense of persisting verities.

We may think of the creed in terms of the church's task of perpetuating the truths of God from one generation to another. As such it resembles a ship straining against a heavy sea, lurching first one way and then another, but always pressing ahead. The creed is a natural expression of Christian discipleship as it recognizes the rhythm of the church in gathering and dispersing. It helps the church declare the revealed truth of God to succeeding generations.

Creedal History

"Confessional authority is limited by and derived from the authority of Scripture, which alone remains ultimately and permanently normative" rightly asserts the Chicago Call. "Nevertheless, as the common insight of those who have been illuminated by the Holy Spirit and seek to be the voice of the 'holy catholic church,' a confession should serve as a guide for the interpretation of Scripture." Thus are we cast into the historical dimension of the creed and especially as it relates to the Scriptures.

John Kelly introduces the subject: "There is plenty of evidence in the New Testament to show that the faith was already beginning to harden into conventional summaries. Creeds in the true meaning of the Word were yet to come, but the movement towards formulation and fixity was under way."[8] Kelly elaborates by reference to the creed-like slogans and tags, catchwords consecrated by popular usage, and longer passages that reflect a community tradition.

Paul's reference "Jesus is Lord" (1 Cor. 12:3) is a case in point. It appears to have been a common confession in the church reflecting the Lord's own teaching and a consensus of conviction. The new convert simply joined his voice with others in confessing Jesus as Lord.

The creed ought not to compete with the Scripture for our loyalty. Each plays a different and complementary role. "The Bible is the Word of God to man," Philip Schaff reminded us, while "the Creed is man's answer to God."[9] The former is God's sure Word to us, and the latter our effort to summarize some portion of what He has said.

Here the Chicago Call reminds us to strike a proper balance. While we should not set up the creeds as a separate source of authority, neither ought we to disregard them as useful résumés of Christian belief or guides to better understanding of the Scriptures.

The creed recalls what the church has for the most part held to be true. It should never be viewed as exhaustive or final (in the sense that we embrace the Scriptures as our ultimate authority in matters of faith and practice). The creed sets the direction and perimeters of our endeavor. It eliminates certain options and points us toward a profitable course of further theological endeavor.

The creed thus provides us with a fallible key to the Scriptures. And while fallible, *it is not as vulnerable to the unhistorical interpretations that plague highly individualized efforts.*

The golden age of the creeds extended over the first five centuries. It included the Apostles', Nicene, and Chalcedonian Creeds. The basic feature of this creedal activity was to express accurately the common experience of Christians.

We may consider the Trinitarian confession as a prime case in point. The essential outline of Trinitarian faith can be seen in the baptismal formula: " 'Go therefore and make disciples of all the nations, baptizing them in the name of the Father and the Son and the Holy Spirit' " (Matt. 28:19, NASB). Christians had experienced God as a solicitous benefactor in the person and work of Christ, and in the fellowship of believers as gathered by the Holy Spirit. This was and is normative for the Christian experience. In five centuries of creedal endeavor, the baptismal core had assumed the refined form we repeat as *The Apostles' Creed.*

Creedal activity continued at a diminished rate until we came to the era of the confessions, about 1530 through 1700. The Augsburg Confession was issued in 1530, as was the first of the Helvetic Confessions; the Articles of the Church of England were agreed upon in 1552 and subsquently revised in 1571; the creed of Prius IV was published in the year 1564; the last of four Helvetic Confessions dates to 1675.

Some prefer to differentiate sharply between confessions and creeds. For instance, Routley argues that confessions "differ from creeds chiefly in being characteristic of an age in which the unity of the visible church was precisely not the primary assumption. A confession becomes the manifesto of a communion which wishes to make clear its differences from another, or from all others."[10] There is merit to what he says, but it tends to obscure what the later confessions have in common with the earlier creeds.

"A Confession of Faith is a Confession of *the one, holy, catholic, and apostolic church,*" Cochrane observes. "It is not the confession of an individual theologian, of a party within the church, or even of a particular denomination or group of denominations. It speaks for the whole church to the whole church."[11] The confession calls for the church to rally to its cry or justify its reason for not doing so. It is no less than the creed an appeal "for the whole church to the whole church."

We cannot, strictly speaking, claim that the confessions lapsed at the turn of the eighteenth century. The Barmen Declaration of 1934 is a notable exception, which laid the foundation for the confessing church in its struggle against the Nazi's effort to turn the German church into an instrument of its policy. In true confessional spirit, the Barmen Declaration called upon the church to resist the German Christian church movement as a repudiation of the church it meant to represent.

The Lausanne Covenant of 1975 also deserves to be included among confessional literature. An illustrative excerpt reads: "We affirm our belief in the one eternal God, Creator and Lord of the world, Father, Son and Holy Spirit, who governs all things according to the purpose of his will. He has been calling out from the world a people for himself, and sending his people back into the world to be his servants and his witnesses, for the extension of his kingdom, the building up of Christ's body, and the glory of his name."[12] The statement was prefaced with an invitation to those who could conscientiously sign the covenant to do so "as an individual member of the body of Christ."

"We affirm the abiding value of the great ecumenical creeds and the Reformation confessions," the Chicago Call states, reviewing the ground we have so briefly covered. "Since such statements are historically and culturally conditioned, however, the church today needs to express its faith afresh, without defecting from the truths apprehended in the past." The old confession is but the starting point of the new; the new confession seeks only to clarify the old in connection with some current issue.

We cannot turn back the historical process to an earlier chapter, as if no events had intervened. The ecumenical creeds and Reformation confessions may guide us, but they cannot assume our responsibility for setting forth abiding truth for our day. The creedal obligation still remains with us as it has upon past generations of Christians.

The Task

The Chicago Call states the task in these words: "We need to articulate our witness against the idolatries and false ideologies of our day." It remains for us to weigh the meaning of this solemn injunction.

1. *The confessional responsibility is personal.* The "we" who articulate incorporates various individuals. Each person stands

as if alone before God to make his confession of faith as his very own, without qualification or accommodation.

Peter confessed Jesus to be " '. . . the Christ, the Son of the living God' " (Matt. 16:16, NASB), but the Lord had previously inquired (v. 13) as to who persons thought Him to be. " 'Some say John the Baptist; some, Elijah; and others, Jeremiah, or one of the prophets,' " the disciples reported (v. 14). He said to them, ". . . 'But who do *you* say that I am?' " (v. 15, italics added). Here Peter assumed the initiative, perhaps to speak for the rest, but at the very least for himself, and confessed Jesus as the Christ. A confession must always have that personal dimension to validate it.

2. *The confessional responsibility is also corporate.* The individual Christian exists in community. ". . . We are to grow up in all aspects unto Him, who is the head, even Christ," Paul admonished, "from whom the whole body, being fitted and held together by that which every joint supplies, according to the proper working of each individual part, causes the growth of the body for the building up of itself in love" (Eph. 4:15, 16, NASB).

Confession contributes to the maturing church. It helps us examine the situation, accept our obligations, and chart a course of action. Thus we affirm our commitment and face the inevitable consequences.

Confession is also a mark of the maturing church. When we learn to share our convictions with fellow believers and confess them before others, the church is coming of age.

3. *The confessional responsibility is continual.* "We affirm the need in our time for a confessing church," admits the Chicago Call. The former creeds and confessions are preambles to the present confessional obligation. As we have received from others, so must we appropriate for ourselves and pass on the heritage to our spiritual posterity.

The past cannot speak for us because we face a contemporary challenge. Whatever the similarity between our age and another, each is distinct and calls for a particular confessional stance. Repetition alone will not suffice for a responsible confessionalism.

Charles Wesley wrote:

> To serve the present age,
> My calling to fulfill—
> O may it all my pow'rs engage
> To do my Master's will!
> —"A Charge to Keep I Have"

The "present age" sets the perimeter for our confessional service, and it is a demanding endeavor that draws heavily upon our resources. Here, in the present, we confess Christ—or not at all.

4. *The confessional responsibility is Christian.* Dietrich Bonhoeffer wrote: "Discipleship without Jesus Christ is a way of our own choosing. It may be the ideal way. It may even lead to martyrdom, but it is devoid of all promise. Jesus will certainly reject it."[13] We could easily substitute the word *confession* for *discipleship* and the commentary would equally apply. Either Christ mediates our confession or he rejects it.

Earlier we considered Christ as the object of our confession and that is true, but here we emphasize Christ as the mediator of our confession. He makes the confession possible in that it is a response to His grace and by His grace. We speak because He has bid us do so and promised to sustain us in the undertaking: "you shall even be brought before governors and kings for My sake, as a testimony to them and to the Gentiles," Jesus warned. "But when they deliver you up, do not become anxious about how or what you will speak; for it shall be given you in that hour what you are to speak" (Matt. 10:18,19, NASB).

5. *The confessional responsibility is verbal.* This fact may seem obvious but ever so many persons seem willing to settle for the idea that "my life is my witness." The perspective has also been refined and promoted with the concept of "Christian-presence." "The basic principle of this approach is that it is the

Christian's main responsibility simply to be present with the man of another faith, perceiving their common humanity with the common needs, feelings, and longings."[14] At best, the Christian-presence ideology reminds us that our life must match our confession of faith; at worst, it becomes an excuse for neglecting our confessional obligation.

" '. . . Do not be afraid any longer, but go on speaking and do not be silent,' " the Lord instructed Paul, " 'for I am with you, and no man will attack you in order to harm you, for I have many people in this city' " (Acts 18:9,10, NASB). Subsequent generations of Christians have been similarly impressed with the responsibility to articulate their faith, even when this meant to invite persecution.

6. *The confessional responsibility is biblical.* We mean this assertion in two ways. In the first place, the Bible provides us with ample injunction and illustration concerning the practice of confessing one's faith. We can hardly think of ourselves as biblical and disregard our obligation to declare our convictions.

The responsibility is also biblical in the sense that it means to confess only what has in essence been revealed in Scripture. The confession is sort of a commentary on Holy Writ. It draws attention not ultimately to itself, but to the revealed truth of God.

Or, to state the matter differently, the confession is an obedient response to the admonition—"Beloved, do not believe every spirit, but test the spirits to see whether they are from God; because many false prophets have gone out into the world" (1 John 4:1, NASB). It brings the claims of men to the court of Scripture.

7. *The confessional responsibility excludes by its activity.* Paul Fuhrmann writes: "We shall see the creeds as monuments to decisive victories of the Christian faith over inner and outer enemies, that in one way or another endangered its very existence. Let us not forget that Christianity in part defined and strengthened itself by way of contrast and opposition."[15] The creeds identified the enemy and declared war upon it.

The creeds are clearer in regard to what Christians do not believe than what they precisely do hold to. They set the household of faith off at arm's length from "the idolatries and false ideologies" of the time; they only suggest the direction that true faith will travel thereafter.

8. *The confessional responsibility conversely includes through its endeavor.* It rallies those who may not have previously recognized themselves as sharing a common faith. The church *emerges* with the confessional labor. It achieves visibility that may have been badly lacking.

While the confession excludes us from some that have seemed compatible, it produces some surprising Christian colleagues. They come from denominations we may have written off, from life-styles that seem improper, from adversary groups of every variety, to kneel with us at the foot of the cross. Thus are we reminded of the Lord's counsel to Peter: " . . . 'What God has cleansed, no longer consider unholy' " (Acts 10:15, NASB). If God chooses to draw a circle so as to include a Cornelius, who are we to reject him?

9. *The confessional responsibility is prophetic.* That is, it focuses God's concern on some pressing issue. Not all confessions are as pointed as the Barmen Declaration in refusing the efforts of Hitler to manipulate the church for political ends, but this prophetic character of the confession is implied if not expressly stated.

Taking a different theological approach to the subject, the church anticipates from its corporate experience the will of God for man in general. The church is in the vanguard, at the cutting edge, of God's dealing with mankind. It breaks ground for others to follow.

10. *The confessional responsibility invites opposition.* It does so for at least two reasons. The first is that the confession contrasts the will of God with the ways of man. The church must resist the temptation to accept the kingdoms of this world as the kingdom of God, both in regard to itself and elsewhere. And such an uncompromising stance threatens man's cherished ways and solicits negative reaction.

The second reason we may anticipate opposition is that confession points out a higher road than we are anxious to travel. It distinguishes between the options available and reminds us that we often prefer something less than the best of these. Thereby we discover not only that our ways deviate from God's perfect will, but that we deliberately stand at a distance.

The confession may appear as meddling in things that are not strictly speaking the prerogative of the church. It seems to stray too far from the sanctuary and into the market place where we resent and contest its incursion.

Summary

We began our discussion with the pointed claim that Christian faith is creedal. The subsequent elaboration has seemed to bear out that conviction.

We have attempted to steer between the opposite errors of a creedal church that merely recites an inherited faith and a creedless church languishing in a doctrinal vacuum. Thus we assume our confessional responsibility without abusing it.

The creed functions as a means of receiving and transmitting the Christian's faith from generation to generation. It resembles a ship lurching through a heavy sea with shifting cargo. The church steers through troubled waters, resisting paganism and heresy alike, preserving the gospel for each succeeding generation, and calling the people of God to their appointed tasks.

The creedal stirrings may be discovered in the Scriptures themselves, the golden age of the creeds reached during the first five centuries of the church, extensive confessional activity observed from about 1530 through 1700, and confessional examples identified to the present. We concluded that while the ecumenical creeds and Reformation confessions may guide us, they cannot assume our responsibility for setting forth abiding truth for our day. "The creedal obligation still remains with us as it has upon past generations of Christians."

The confessional task is personal, corporate, continual,

Christian, verbal, and biblical; it excludes and includes; it is prophetic; it invites opposition. The list of characteristics are descriptive, not exhaustive. Much more could be said but we run the danger of losing the larger concerns by extending the possibilities further. We have attempted to better understand the nature of confessional responsibility as a necessary step toward assuming our Christian calling.

Notes

1. C. S. Lewis, *Mere Christianity* (London: Fontana, 1952), p. 156.

2. Arthur Cochrane, *The Church's Confession Under Hitler* (Philadelphia: Westminster, 1952), p. 182.

3. Ibid., p. 184.

4. Erik Routley, *Creeds and Confessions* (Philadelphia: Westminster, 1952), p. 131.

5. Cochrane, *Church's Confession,* p. 206.

6. Lesslie Newbigin, *Honest Religion for Secular Man* (Philadelphia: Westminster, 1966), pp. 120–21.

7. Karl Barth, *The Humanity of God* (Richmond: John Knox, 1966), p. 19.

8. John Kelly, *Early Christian Creeds* (London: Longmans, 1960), p. 13.

9. Philip Schaff, The *Creeds of Christendom* (New York: Harper and Row, 1877), p. 3.

10. Routley, *Creeds and Confessions,* p. 6.

11. Cochrane, *Church's Confession,* p. 185.

12. J.D. Douglas, *Let the Earth Hear His Voice* (Minneapolis: World Wide Publication, 1975), p. 3.

13. Dietrich Bonhoeffer, *The Cost of Discipleship* (New York: Macmillan, 1959), p. 640.

14. Owen Thomas, ed., *Attitudes Toward Other Religions* (New York: Harper and Row, 1969), p. 26.

15. Paul Fuhrmann, *An Introduction to the Great Creeds of the Church* (Philadelphia: Westminster, 1960), pp. 13–14.

6. A Call to Holistic Salvation

by

LANE DENNIS

Lane Dennis is managing editor for Cornerstone Books, a division of Good News Publishers. He is an ordained Presbyterian minister (UPUSA) and author of A Reason For Hope *(Old Tappan: Fleming H. Revell, 1976). A graduate of McCormick Theological Seminary, he is currently a doctoral candidate in religion at Northwestern University.*

We deplore the tendency of evangelicals to understand salvation solely as an individual, spiritual and otherworldly matter to the neglect of the corporate, physical and this-worldly implication of God's saving activity.

Therefore we urge evangelicals to recapture a holistic view of salvation. The witness of Scripture is that because of sin our relationships with God, ourselves, others and creation are broken. Through the atoning work of Christ on the cross, healing is possible for these broken relationships.

Wherever the church has been faithful to its calling, it has proclaimed personal salvation; it has been a channel of God's healing to those in physical and emotional need; it has sought justice for the oppressed and disinherited; and it has been a good steward of the natural world.

As evangelicals we acknowledge our frequent failure to reflect this holistic view of salvation. We therefore call the church to participate fully in God's saving activity through work and prayer, and to strive for justice and liberation for the oppressed, looking forward to the culmination of salvation in the new heaven and new earth to come.

The hallmark of evangelicalism has been its emphasis upon the experience of personal salvation—individual commitment to Jesus Christ as personal Savior. This emphasis is central to any vital experience of Christian faith. But whenever this focus becomes exclusive—i.e., whenever salvation is understood "solely as an individual, spiritual, and otherworldly matter to the neglect of the corporate, physical, and thisworldly"—there is something seriously lacking. In other words, the "Call to Holistic Salvation" points to the debilitating polarization of what should be a "holistic" Christian life embracing the full range of human experience—individual and corporate, spiritual and material, temporal and eternal.

This polarization can, of course, take either of two extremes. On one hand it can take the form of a "temporalized gospel" that sees only the humanity of Jesus and proclaims only a message of political and material salvation. Insofar as this "gospel" has abandoned the spiritual, transcendent dimension found in *Christ,* it offers only the illusion of salvation expressed in human ideology. On the other hand, there are those who attempt to "spiritualize" the gospel out of history and the empirical world. Insofar as this "spiritualized gospel" fails to find at least some concrete expression in time and space, it too would seem to be illusory.

Neither of these extremes could be considered a genuine expression of salvation as affirmed by the historic, biblical faith.[1] Though this conclusion may seem obvious, the far-reaching implications of the problem are not often recognized.

The problem is not simply a matter of achieving a proper *balance* between complementary emphases. Rather we need to recover a consciousness or world-view that recognizes the *interpenetration* and necessary *co-inherence* of those dimensions that have become polarized. Today, however, this challenges the fundamental orientation of Western culture rooted especially in the rationalistic, naturalistic heritage of the Enlightenment. For the prevailing naturalistic consciousness that dominates Western culture not only denies the co-inherence of the temporal and spiritual (or in other words the natural and supernatural); it also denies out of hand the reality of the spiritual-supernatural dimension. For the modern mind the gospel represents an intolerable intellectual scandal.

The issues raised by this situation involve the most fundamental matters of Christian doctrine: the meaning of the Incarnation, the life and work of Jesus Christ, the doctrine of salvation, the mission of the church. If we are to "recapture a holistic view of salvation," we will need to begin by reflecting upon these most basic dimensions of the Christian faith as found in Holy Scripture and proclaimed in word and deed by the church throughout the ages.

The Incarnation

The starting point for understanding the relationship between the material and the spiritual and between the natural and supernatural implications of salvation is the Incarnation. The Incarnation demonstrates that the apparent dualism between time and eternity is overcome in the person of Jesus Christ. As the prologue to John's Gospel proclaims, "The Word became flesh . . ." (John 1:14, NIV): Jesus Christ, the eternally existent Word of God, the One through whom all things were created, became incarnate within our temporal, material, finite order of existence. This is expressed by the Nicene Creed:

> We believe in One Lord Jesus Christ, the only Son of God, eternally begotten of the Father, God from God, light from

light, true God from true God, begotten not made, of one being with the Father. Through Him all things were made. For us and for our salvation he came down from heaven: by the power of the Holy Spirit he became Incarnate from the Virgin Mary, and was made man.

On the most basic level, the Incarnation demonstrates that *there is no reason in principle* why Christian faith must be polarized into spiritual and material, into eternal and temporal. In and through Jesus Christ the dualism is overcome, such that eternal and spiritual realities find concrete expression in space and time. Thus the reality of the Incarnation undercuts the positions of both disincarnate spirituality and finite ideology. It is a scandal that cuts both ways: On one hand it deposes those who reject the ontological reality that Jesus is eternally God—those who therefore end up with a finite "gospel" proclaiming an illusory political and materialist salvation; on the other hand it deposes those who reject the ontological fact demonstrated by the Incarnation that spirituality can (and must) find concrete expression in the temporal order, or else it is little more than a pious illusion.

The Kingdom

The interpenetration and co-inherence of spiritual and temporal is expressed not only by the Incarnation as a *doctrine of the church,* but concretely by the *Incarnation as an event,* that is, in the life and earthly ministry of Jesus Christ. The problem comes into focus in considering the meaning of the kingdom of God as revealed in Jesus' ministry: The repeated misunderstanding of the kingdom—by Jesus' followers as well as his opponents—as proclaimed by Jesus reflects a fundamental misunderstanding of the true relationship between the spiritual and temporal spheres of existence.

The problem must first be seen against the background of the first century and the situation of the Jewish people at that time. Israel was living in a state of political and religious crisis. Politically, Israel was an occupied territory, subjected to the totalitarian rule of the Roman Empire. Religiously, this state of affairs implied an additional crisis as the Jewish people tried to reconcile their faith with the historical tragedy.

How could the glory of Israel be restored and re-established? What could the messianic promises mean in this tragic situation? During the time of Jesus' earthly ministry these questions were never very far from pious Jewish speculation. Though there were a variety of ways in which they were confronted, the problem of the kingdom was probably taken most seriously within two more or less distinct schools of thought.

On one hand there were the Zealots with their zeal for the law and a revolutionary socio-political program.[2] On the other hand there was a loosely defined apocalyptic school with a radically dualistic world-view and exotic speculations about an imminent cataclysmic end to the present age.[3] In other words, the Zealots attempted to *temporalize* the kingdom of God and God's saving activity into a program of social political revolution; the Apocalypticists tended to spiritualize the kingdom out of present human history.[4]

The meaning of the kingdom in Jesus' life and ministry stands in contrast to both of these extremes.[5] In the first place we must recognize that the meaning of the kingdom is central to Jesus' whole ministry and mission, and therefore to the meaning of salvation in Jesus Christ. In the Gospel of Luke, for example, Jesus begins his public ministry in the temple at Nazareth by reading from the messianic passage in Isaiah (61:1-2; 58:6) and then stating that "Today this scripture is fulfilled in your hearing" (Luke 4:21, NIV). In other words Jesus is the Messiah, the One sent by God for the express purpose of proclaiming the Good News of the kingdom of God (Luke 4:43).[6]

Secondly, we see that the kingdom of God clearly has present, temporal implications. For example, in casting out demons Jesus explained that "if it is by the Spirit of God that I cast out demons, then the kingdom of God has come upon you" (Matt. 12:28; cf. Luke 11:20). Similarly, in the healing ministry of Jesus and His disciples, the kingdom and healing were shown to be intimately related (Matt. 9:35; 4:23; 10:7,8;

Luke 10:9). In each of these cases, and in contrast to the spiritualized understanding of the apocalypticists, we see that in some sense the kingdom of God is present in history, and that the specific features of the apocalyptic new age are breaking into present reality. In Jesus' own ministry, then, the kingdom of God had dramatic temporal consequences, bringing healing and wholeness to the broken minds and bodies of those in the present world order.

Thirdly, Jesus specifically rejected Apocalypticism, for example, in his response to the Pharisees' question about foretelling when the kingdom would come. ". . . 'The kingdom of God,' Jesus replied, 'is not coming with signs to be observed; nor will they say, "Lo, here it is!" "or "There!" for behold, the kingdom of God is in the midst of you' " (Luke 17:20,21). Thus Jesus rejected the popular pastime "in Jewish apocalyptic circles of watching for and calculating the signs that the End was at hand"[7] (a pastime, we might add, which has become popular again today).

Since Jesus rejected a spiritualized religion, the temptation of some has been to see Him as a Zealotist revolutionary.[8] In support of this position a wide range of evidence is cited: Jesus was condemned by Rome for the crime of sedition; the inscription on the cross read "The King of the Jews"; Jesus was crucified with two apparently Zealotist criminals; at least one and possibly two other disciples were or had once been Zealots;[9] Jesus was severely critical of the social and religious order, as were the Zealots also.

But the conclusion that Jesus was a Zealot can be reached only by excluding the clear evidence to the contrary, and only by misunderstanding the true nature of Jesus' messianic mission. In fact the story of the temptation seems to suggest that political messianism was the greatest threat and temptation to Jesus' true mission. (Matt. 4:8–11). Similarly, Jesus' association with tax collectors and sinners (Matt. 11:19) and His answer to the question concerning taxation (Mark 12:13–17; Matt. 22:15–22; Luke 20:20–26) certainly would not have been acceptable to a Zealot.

Finally, Jesus' proclamation of the kingdom must be distinguished from Zealotist expectations by the fact that it included the idea that the kingdom ultimately transcends the limits of space and time. In other words, Jesus taught that the kingdom of God would be consummated only in the "age to come" where the faithful would inherit an eternal life filled with blessing in the presence of God (Mark 10:17–31).[10]

Over against Apocalyptic spiritualization, Jesus demonstrated that the saving work of God is active on the plane of human history bringing healing and wholeness in the midst of sin and death. In other words, the new age, the kingdom of God, has already broken into the present, even if only in a fragmentary way. Over against Zealotist temporalization, however, Jesus pointed to the fulfillment of the kingdom at the end of time when the final victory will be established. The Zealotist hope in the quest of radicalism was not radical enough; the oppression, which seems to be only social or political, is rooted in something much deeper—in the human heart and the fallen nature of this present world order.

The biblical meaning of both the Incarnation and the kingdom of God demonstrates that *there is no reason in principle why Christian faith and salvation should be polarized; for in and through Jesus Christ the dualism is resolved.* Yet in the Christian's life and the witness of the church it has not always been easy to maintain this unity. To understand this problem we need to look further into the meaning of salvation, especially in terms of the historic, biblical Christian teaching concerning the atoning work of Christ and the means by which we may be saved.

Holistic Salvation: Biblical Teaching

A comprehensive treatment of the historic, biblical doctrine of salvation would be a gargantuan task—much more than we could begin to accomplish in these few pages. Here we can only touch upon a few dimensions and perhaps raise a few important issues. Thus we shall limit the discussion to a brief treatment of only three themes, i.e., the biblical teachings on *justification, sanctification,* and *reconcilation.*

Justification

What then is the biblical meaning of *justification?* "According to original biblical usage . . . , 'justification' must be defined as a *declaring just by court order.*" [11] In the Old Testament, justification draws upon the idea of a divine act of judgment, as in the main sense of declaring just in a court of judgment. Thus "a forensic conception is without doubt basic here in as much as the image is taken from the context of judical trial, with man appearing before God as the defendant."[12]

How then does the sinner, standing before a just and holy God, become justified? In the writing of the apostle Paul this is explained in no uncertain terms. We "are justified by his [God's] grace as a gift, through the redemption which is in Christ Jesus, whom God put forward as an expiation by his blood, to be received by faith . . ." (Rom. 3:24,25). The sole basis for our justification according to Paul is God's gracious gift of what has been accomplished on our behalf by the atoning work of Jesus Christ on the cross, received by the sinner in faith.[13] Moreover, there is nothing that we can do to justify ourselves through our own efforts or "works." For " . . . a man is not justified by works of the law but through faith in Jesus Christ . . . because by works of the law shall no one be justified" (Gal. 2:16).[14]

If we claim to represent the historic, biblical doctrine of justification, what has been said so far must be affirmed without qualification. But if we were to leave the discussion at this point, we would have dealt with only part of the question, presented only half the truth, and left ourselves open to serious misunderstanding. For such a "one-sided" reading might suggest that there is no relationship between faith and works, that we are advocating antinomianism, that justification is "merely" forensic, that it represents "merely" a change in status without a corresponding ontological change in reality.

A careful reading of Paul, however, does not permit these conclusions. In the first place, Paul is not opposed to doing good works. When Paul set faith and the righteousness of faith over against works (e.g., Rom. 3:28), it is against *the works of the*

Law (i.e., works done for the purpose of trying to "legally" justify oneself before God), not against works done in and out of faith.[15] To the contrary, Paul stresses the importance of "bearing fruit in every good work" (Col. 1:10), because Jesus Christ "gave himself for us to redeem us from all iniquity and to purify for himself a people of his own who are zealous for good deeds" (Titus 2:14). In other words, there is an organic, necessary relationship between justification and good works.

Similarly, we cannot conclude that justification is "merely" forensic, i.e., that we have been "merely" declared righteous contrary to actually being made righteous—at least in some sense. The change that takes place in justification involves not only a change in status. We agree, of course, with Paul that God imputes righteousness without good works (Rom. 4:6). But when this "imputation" is the work of God it is not "mere imputation." It involves a change in reality. When God declares on the basis of faith that we are just (righteous), His Word accomplishes what is spoken.[16] For the Word of God is not merely "talk"; when God speaks, worlds come into being, and the dead are raised to life. The Word of God includes the power to accomplish what is declared. Thus we must agree with Paul that justification involves a transformation or re-creation: "For we are his workmanship, *created* in Christ Jesus for good works . . ." (Eph. 2:10, italics added); "Therefore, if any one is in Christ, he is a new creation . . ." (2 Cor. 5:17).

It is a distortion of Paul's teaching on justification to emphasize only faith, or what we might call "mere faith." The sole basis for justification is of course what Christ has done on the cross, received by faith. *But what is this faith?* It is a *living faith* created for and necessarily resulting in good works; it is a *living faith* rooted in the ontological change in status *and state,* though this change in state is still in the process of being appropriated experientially as the believer grows in faith (2 Cor. 10:15) and works out his own salvation with fear and trembling (Phil. 2:12).

In comparing the Epistle of James with the Pauline corpus, it would seem at first glance that basic differences exist. Whereas Paul wrote ". . . a man is justified by faith apart from works . . ." (Rom. 3:28), in clear contrast James said, ". . . a man is justified by works and not by faith alone" (James 2:24). Even the same Old Testament example is used by both apostles in coming to their apparently opposite conclusions.

But again a superficial reading results in a "one-sided" conclusion.[17] The Pauline argument begins with Abraham's initial faith acceptance of God's promise before Abraham had done any "works"; Abraham was reckoned righteous simply because he believed God (Rom. 4:3; see also Gen. 15:6). James, however, starts not from Abraham's initial moment of faith (Gen. 15:6), but from a point much later in his life (Gen. 22) where the reference is to Abraham's willingness to offer his son Isaac: "Was not Abraham our father justified by works, when he offered his son Isaac upon the altar" (James 2:21). But what is this "work," this "act of faith," which Abraham performs? James gives the surprising answer that it is actually the *fulfillment* of what went before when ". . . 'Abraham believed God, and it was reckoned to him as righteousness' . . ." (James 2:23). Similarly, James says that ". . . faith was active along with . . . works . . ." (James 2:22), which indicates works neither preceded faith nor caused faith; and that "faith was completed by works" (James 2:22), which indicates that faith that does not produce "works" is "incomplete," or in other words, ineffectual and dead (James 2:26).

In the end Paul and James were agreed: both affirmed an inner cohesion of faith and works. As seen in the example of Abraham, the seeming conflict arises out of the fact that Paul and James were approaching the same question of justification from different directions. Paul had started with the "moment" of faith and moved to the life of faith that necessarily follows; James had focused first upon the life of faith as it is revealed in righteousness, emphasizing that "works" are the necessary consequence of genuine faith, of justification already having taken place. "In short, James's point was [that] true faith is not dead, empty or fruitless"[18]—to which Paul would agree. Faith and works are homogeneous, woven together into the totality of life. Where this is not the case, genuine faith does not exist.

Sanctification

Though we have delayed the mention of sanctification until this point, we could not avoid dealing with the question of holy living as part of the discussion on justification; for "justification and sanctification are inseparable, [just as] a faith divorced from good works is not the faith that justifies."[19] Justification must in some sense include sanctification while not being identical with it; conversely, sanctification must in some sense include justification while not being identical with it.

In emphasizing as we did above that justification was not a "legal fiction"—i.e., that an ontological change in status *and state* actually takes place—this *change in state* might best be described as consisting in at least one aspect of sanctification. Where justification has taken place it is realized in the form of sanctification; conversely, wherever sanctification happens in human lives it is the necessary result of the divine activity founded upon justification.

The same cohesion that exists between faith and works exists in like manner between justification and sanctification. To paraphrase James, we may say that we are in some sense "justified by our sanctification" if by this we mean that sanctification is the fulfillment of what justification accomplishes, thereby demonstrating to the world that justification is operative. As with faith and works there is a necessary inner co-inherence between justification and sanctification.

In addition to this, other dimensions of sanctification need to be considered, though we can do little more than mention some of these here. First, sanctification can never be thought of as an automatically and mechanically realized result of justification—as something that happens without our own cooperation.[20] To be sure, justification is the result of *God's* activity, of God's grace, but it happens nonetheless only with our free and intentional participation. Thus, while God is the source of salvation, the believer (if he is truly such) is an active, intentional participant in its realization, as the imperatives of Scripture clearly indicate (e.g., Rom. 6:13,19; 8:13; 2 Cor. 7:1; etc.).

Secondly, sanctification involves what we might call three "moments" of realization—past, present, and future. There is a sense in which *we have already been sanctified* as when Paul said ". . . you were washed, you were sanctified, you were justified . . ." (1 Cor. 6:11; cf. 1 Cor. 1:2); similarly, in union with Christ in his death and resurrection, we are (already) "dead to sin" and "alive to God" (Rom. 6:1–11). Then there is a sense in which *we are being sanctified,* as when Paul wrote that we ". . . are being changed into his likeness from one degree of glory to another . . ." (2 Cor. 3:18). Likewise there is also a sense in which *we will be sanctified,* a sense in which the goal we strive after lies in the future (Phil. 3:12–14) when at the appearing of Christ the faithful will receive the "crown of righteousness" (2 Tim. 4:7,8).[21]

Finally, sanctification needs to be seen in relationship to the church. Neither sanctification nor justification happen in isolation, but rather in and through the body of Christ by the working of the Holy Spirit. Thus Paul wrote:

> So then you are no longer strangers and sojourners, but you are fellow citizens with the saints and members of the household of God, built upon the foundation of the apostles and prophets, Christ Jesus himself being the cornerstone, in whom the whole structure is joined together and grows into a holy temple in the Lord; in whom you also are built into it for a dwelling place of God in the Spirit (Eph. 2:19–22).

Similarly, Paul wrote that Christ gave himself up *for the church* ". . . that he might sanctify her . . . that she might be holy . . ." (Eph. 5:25–27). Sanctification therefore involves participation in the body of Christ with continuing growth into ministry, unity, maturity, and "the fullness of Christ" (Eph. 4:11–13).

Reconciliation

Much of what has already been said concerning the relationship between justification and sanctification anticipates the discussion of reconciliation, for the doctrines of justification and reconciliation are also inseparable. As with sanctification, reconciliation relates to the ontological change in state that has been accomplished in justification.

In reconciliation the estrangement and alienation existing between God and man as a consequence of sin is overcome—wherever the atoning work of Christ is accepted in saving faith. Again, this is not a "fictional" change, but rather a change in reality that has in some sense already been accomplished. As the apostle Paul wrote, ". . . through our Lord Jesus Christ . . . we have now received our reconciliation" (Rom. 5:11). But as with sanctification there is also a present and future sense. Thus, we are admonished "on behalf of Christ, [to] be reconciled . . ." (2 Cor. 5:20), indicating that the work of reconciliation is not yet completed and that our intentional cooperation is necessary. Similarly, we have the hope of the fulfillment of reconciliation when all things shall be reconciled to Christ (Col. 1:20; Eph. 1:10) and brought in subjection to His eternal reign (Heb. 2:8; 10:12,13).

While reconciliation is based upon justification as established through the atoning work of Christ, it is also directly related to sanctification. One of the purposes of reconciliation is to produce sanctification. Though we were once hostile and estranged from God, Paul wrote, we have been ". . . reconciled in his body of flesh by his death, *in order to [be presented] . . . holy and blameless and irreproachable before him*" (Col. 1:21,22, italics added).[22]

Finally, in the doctrine of reconciliation we are given a glimpse into the all encompassing goal of reconciliation accomplished, but still to be fully realized, through the atoning work of Christ. In the most basic sense reconciliation restores the relationship of God to man. But the consequences of sin are not limited only to this relationship; the whole of creation has been affected by sin, and therefore by alienation and estrangement from the Creator. The reconciliation that Christ accomplishes starts between God and man, but from there it reaches out to the whole cosmos.

Moreover, those who have been reconciled have been given "the ministry of reconciliation" (2 Cor. 5:18)—the privilege and obligation to be God's ambassadors of reconciliation, to participate in God's reconciling activity within the whole cosmic sphere of God's saving activity. We are therefore given the task of reconciliation between ourselves and others.

The paradigm for this level of reconciliation is what Christ has accomplished in closing the seemingly unbridgeable gap between Jew and Gentile (Eph. 2:12–17). If this archetypal form of alienation between races has been overcome, there is no reason that every form of human division cannot be overcome in and through Christ. But even where this is accomplished, the alienating effects of sin within the cosmic order of existence need to be overcome. Thus the atonement becomes the means by which all things in heaven and earth are finally reconciled to Christ. "For in him," the apostle Paul wrote, "all the fulness of God was pleased to dwell, and through him to reconcile to himself all things, whether on earth or in heaven, making peace by the blood of his cross" (Col. 1:19,20; see also Eph. 1:9,10).

Holistic Salvation: Breakdown and Recovery

What stands out most clearly in the discussion of these three dimensions of salvation is the *organic, necessary unity* between a whole range of complementary concepts: for example, between justification and sanctification; between belief and righteousness; between faith and works; between God's work and our cooperation; between a change in status and an ontological change in state; between a spiritual conversion and a concrete change in life; between justification and reconciliation; between reconciliation with God and reconciliation with others and the cosmos; between the individual and the corporate; and so on. We see then that insofar as there is an evangelical tendency "to understand salvation solely as an individual, spiritual and otherworldly matter to the neglect of the corporate, physical and this-worldly," this tendency is related to the most basic theological issues.

Seen from another perspective, however, this is still part of a larger problem. For it is not just that the full meaning of salvation has somehow become reduced; rather the problem is bound up in something much more comprehensive—that the prevailing consciousness of Western culture makes it extremely difficult to affirm a holistic world-view in which the spiritual and the eternal co-inhere, such as the historic, biblical Christian understanding of reality requires.

In short the modern consensus is that we live in a one-dimensional world—the reductionist reality of naturalism, positivism, and materialism. In reaction to this, we evangelicals have tried to affirm the existence of the eternal-spiritual dimension, but we have often done so without a clear understanding of the problem and have ended up fighting the battle by our opponents' ground rules. In the process we have often lost the proper understanding of the temporal-material dimension, with the result that the holistic-Christian meaning of salvation and the holistic-Christian world-view have become fragmented.

The problem, I would suggest, grows out of the whole development of Western culture, especially as this can be seen in the late medieval breakdown of Western Christendom and the emergence of Reformation Protestantism. Though we cannot, of course, replay the Reformation and its causes in the few pages that remain, we need at least to recognize some of the issues that took shape at that time, for they are at the heart of the problem.

There is general agreement that the beginning of the modern Western consciousness is rooted in the Scholasticism of the high Middle Ages. Clearly the most important development of the time was the rediscovery of classical Greek philosophy in the twelfth century by the medieval Scholastics. As Aristotelian writings in particular were recovered and translated, a whole new world of philosophy was thrust upon the Christianized culture of the West. Though this new world of philosophy was uncomfortably at variance with the theology of the times, its brilliance could not be denied. Thus through painstaking analysis, argument, and synthesis, the Scholastics undertook to reconcile Christian and Greek thought.

The impact upon the intellectual climate was immediate and extensive. "By 1255," historian Francis Oakley writes, "the faculty of arts curriculum at Paris included the whole corpus of Aristotle's writings. Henceforth, no other current thinker could rival his prestige. He was now simply 'the philosopher.' He was the great authority on whom budding philosophers and natural scientists were required to cut their intellectual teeth. His were the philosophical categories in terms of which professional theologians were trained to think, and with his scheme of things medievals struggled henceforth to harmonize their Christian beliefs."[23]

Within little more than one hundred years, Aristotelianism had left its indelible mark upon Christian theology. Thus in a brilliant but problematic synthesis, St. Thomas Aquinas (1225–1274) achieved a "thoroughgoing assimilation of Aristotelian rationalism in general and Aristotle's philosophy of nature in particular."[24] Whether positively or negatively, St. Thomas's synthesis has affected all of subsequent theology in the West.

Most problematic for the biblical Christian's understanding of the world was the Thomistic assimilation of Aristotle's naturalism and his naturalistic theory of causality. This took the form first of natural theology, which St. Thomas considered fully sufficient with respect to understanding the material world, and even for arriving at certain Christian doctrines such as the existence of God. St. Thomas still held, however, that the blessed truths of the Christian faith such as the Trinity and the sacraments could only be understood with the aid of divine grace.[25] The effect, nevertheless, was that the tip of a wedge began to separate nature and grace, that is the temporal and eternal dimensions of existence. From this point henceforth, the separation increased until any hope of unity was surrendered, and the one-dimensional consciousness of naturalism, positivism, and materialism came to dominate Western culture.[26]

Concurrent with these theological developments, the Western church was also experiencing problematic changes in practice. First, we must acknowledge, however, the monumental achievements of the medieval church: which transformed the entire Western European continent bringing civilization out of barbarism and Christianity out of paganism; which gave us the magnificent achievements of the high Middle Ages as exemplified by the hundreds of matchless cathedrals throughout Europe; which gave birth to an entire culture reflecting (though of course imperfectly) the biblical, Christian consciousness.[27] By the late Middle Ages, however, much of the Western church was in a state of rapid decline, characterized by a marked deterioration in morality, the widespread practice of simony, a bloated bureaucracy, and so on. The most infamous abuse—the one that triggered the Reformation—was of course the widespread practice of selling indulgences. It is this latter abuse that is most important for our discussion since it points to a much broader problem. For the selling of indulgences is only one aspect of the church's general move toward turning Christian faith into a commodity that could be bought and sold, dispensed in the sacraments, or otherwise transmitted by mechanical ministrations.

Though "Christian Aristotelianism" and the breakdown of Western Christianity may seem far removed, they share a common theme: The movement toward the "materialization" or "objectification" of the Christian faith—in Thomism via Arisotelian naturalism, and in the practice of the church via a "mechanization" of salvation. In protest against this trend, Martin Luther and the Reformation in general called for the recovery of true spirituality, emphasizing that salvation was something obtained through faith alone, rather than being a commodity to be bought and sold in indulgences, or dispensed through magical rites or the objectified ministrations of a religious bureaucracy. The Reformation emphasis opposed any religious forms that would tend to undercut the principle of true spirituality as expressed in the doctrine of *sola fide.* In short, the Reformers opposed any religious practice that might become ossified into objectified lifeless forms.

Among the leading Reformers, this program was carried through most consistently under Zwingli in Northern Switzerland. Thus, Zwingli bitterly attacked the established ecclesiastical structure for obtaining salvation through a religious system of "works"; under his direction religious statuary and images were destroyed because of their idolatrous nature; every interpretation of the actual presence of Christ in the Eucharist was rejected in favor of a purely symbolic interpretation; and at one point even the use of musical intruments and singing were eliminated from worship. Of the leading reformers, Zwingli carried through the principle of spirituality most consistently by opposing any and all objectified, formalized expressions of Christianity. Here then is the logical conclusion of a thoroughgoing spiritualism: If the sole basis for true religion is *spiritual,* then any attempt to embody this in concrete forms becomes idolatrous.

Out of this background two basic principles are clearly evident: On the one hand there is the Roman Catholic principle that emphasizes the material, objective dimensions of religion—a principle that came to be seriously abused in the late Middle Ages; on the other hand there is the Protestant principle emphasizing the spiritual, subjective dimensions of religion. On the basis of the spiritual-subjective principle, Protestants criticize Catholics for advocating a lifeless formalism, works-type righteousness, idolatrous adoration of images, a mechanical sacramentalism, etc. Conversely, on the basis of the objective principle, Catholics criticize Protestants for advocating an illusory "faith" without form, antinomian spirituality, arrogant individualism, and sectarianism.

While there is unfortunately some truth in both the Protestant and Catholic *critiques,* there is also truth in both the Protestant and Catholic *principles.* The answer is not to jettison either the objective or the subjective dimensions of Christianity; it is not that either of the two principles are *inherently* wrong, but that they are open to abuse and valid only in organic relationship to their complementary opposite. In order for the objective forms to be valid, they must be rooted in the grace of God received through faith—even through faith alone—if this is properly understood as a living faith rather than "mere" faith. However encumbered Catholic theology may sometimes have become, this truth was clearly affirmed in Catholic tradition (for example by Origin, Hilary, Basel, Chrysostom, Augustine, Cyril of Alexandria, and especially Ambrosiaster and Bernard[28]) and even by St. Thomas. Thus commenting on 1 Timothy 1:8, St. Thomas wrote: "We know that the law is good, if one uses it lawfully. . . . [But] the law was given that sin might be known, for if the law did not say, 'You shall not covet,' I should not have known what it is to covet (Rom. 7:7), as the *commandments* teach. *There is therefore no hope of justification in them, but in faith alone.* We hold that a man is justified by faith without the works of the law (Rom. 3:28)."[29]

Similarly, except in the most extreme forms, Protestantism has not jettisoned the objective principle altogether; for in order for faith to be anything more than illusion, it must find some concrete expression. Thus, virtually every Protestant denomination assumes the validity of objective ecclesiastical structures, emphasizes that faith must be realized in life, stresses the importance of works of love growing out of faith, and accepts the value of formal expressions of piety in music and some form of "liturgy." Even where the sacraments are considered to be only symbolic (or spiritual), it would seem that it is impossible to hold that they are "merely" symbolic. In other words, we all must affirm at minimum that the sacraments (e.g., the Lord's Supper and Baptism) bear witness to the atoning work of Jesus Christ.

But what do we mean by this? Do we mean that the sacraments *merely* bear witness, or they *effectually* bear witness? If they effectually bear witness, then it is because of the reality that they make present (when perceived in faith). If the sacraments *actually do* bear witness, then it is because of what *God* accomplishes in and through them, or, in other words, because of God's active presence in and through them.[30] In this sense even a Baptist tacitly affirms that the grace of God is present in and through the sacraments insofar as they are effectually able, by the grace of God, to bear witness to the saving work of Jesus Christ.[31]

It is impossible for Christianity to be genuine without affirming both the objective-material dimension and the subjective-spiritual dimension of Christian truth—even though either of these dimensions is sometimes not fully recognized. Faith without form is just as "dead" as form without faith. Unfortunately, it is too common that we have a partial or distorted understanding of either dimension, and, therefore, of both dimensions.

Though we started with what may have seemed a secondary problem in evangelical theology, we have seen that it involves Christian faith and practice in the most basic way. Recapturing a "holistic view of salvation," as the Chicago Call puts it, involves recovering the heart of the gospel as reflected in the Incarnation, the earthly ministry of Jesus Christ, and his atoning work on the cross. If we truly believe in these, it is impossible to "understand salvation solely as an individual, spiritual and otherworldly matter to the neglect of the corporate, physical and this-worldly." For the Word has become flesh and dwelt among us; the kingdom has broken into history; God's saving activity is present in the world bringing healing, hope, and ultimately salvation to the broken minds and bodies living in this age.

Similarly, the meaning of salvation as reflected in the inseparable doctrines of justification, sanctification, and reconciliation precludes the polarization of the gospel into faith versus works, individual versus corporate, reconciliation with God versus reconciliation with others and with the cosmos.

There is rather, in the heart of the gospel, a necessary unity that binds these together.

Finally, we have seen that the problem is rooted in the basic development of Western culture as it took shape in the late Middle Ages and the Reformation; and that any solution will have to transcend both Catholic and Protestant reductionism, recovering the proper co-inherence of the objective-material and the subjective-spiritual as affirmed by the historic, biblical Christian faith. We will have to affirm *both* the absolute necessity of the spiritual dimension of faith *and* the equally necessary material dimension by demonstrating that God is (and must be) incarnate in the life, order, worship, sacraments, and praxis of the church.

In the end there is no valid theological basis for the polarization of Christian faith and practice; it is rather a fundamental distortion of the meaning of the gospel. Recovering a holistic view of salvation, then, implies the recovery of the historic, biblical faith—including the valid insights of Catholicism and Protestantism, and the witness of the church throughout the ages. This is to say that the Word must once again become flesh in our own lives as part of the body of Christ and thereby carry the transforming presence of Jesus Christ into the whole of human affairs.

Notes

1. These extremes do not normally exist in any "pure" form. They are presented here as "ideal types" (in the sense of Max Weber's usage) or "typological constructs" for the purpose of clarifying the analysis. The primary features of these polar extremes are nonetheless evidenced, in varying degrees, within Christendom; i.e., we could identify fairly obvious expressions of these in the real world, though they would never be fully consistent with the ideal typology.

2. For a comprehensive analysis of Zealotism, see Martin Hengel, *Die Zeloten* (Leiden: E.J. Brill, 1961); a more popular and highly readable treatment is offered by Martin Hengel in *Was Jesus a Revolutionist?* trans. William Klassen (Philadelphia: Fortress Press, 1971) and by Oscar Cullman in *Jesus and the Revolutionaries,* trans. Gareth Put-

nam (New York: Harper and Row, 1970). Each of these foregoing studies presents a clear and convincing case for the position that Jesus was not a "revolutionist" nor a Zealot. The opposing opinion is represented especially by S.G.F. Brandon in *Jesus and the Zealots: A Study of The Political Factor in Primitive Christianity* (New York: Scribner's, 1968).

3. For the characteristics of Apocalypticism, see esp., D.S. Russell, *The Method and Message of Jewish Apocalyptic* (Philadelphia: Westminster Press, 1964), p. 14; W.O.E. Oesterley, *The Books of the Apocrypha* (London: Robert Scott, 1915), pp. 100–10; Klaus Kock, *The Rediscovery of Apocalyptic*, trans. Margaret Kohl (Naperville, Ill.: Alex R. Allenson, 1972), pp. 28–33; George Eldon Ladd, *A Theology of the New Testament* (Grand Rapids: Eerdmans, 1974), p. 61; and *The Presence of the Future* (Grand Rapids: Eerdmans, 1974), pp. 76–101.

4. This is, of course, an oversimplification, but nonetheless useful for analysis. Implied by this approach is the idea that Zealotism is a concrete example of a "temporalized gospel" and that Apocalypticism is a concrete example of a "spiritualized gospel." It should be kept in mind, however, that insofar as "temporalization" and "spiritualization" are "ideal constructs," the empirical expressions of these constructs never correspond fully to the ideal. (Cf. note 1 above.) Qumran, at the time of the fall of Jerusalem, is a case that illustrates the problem: For example, should Qumran be seen as strictly apocalyptic or was it actually militaristic? Scholarship is divided on the issue. The most convincing scholarly opinion seems to suggest that the Qumran community may have gone through a series of developmental stages. See esp., E.J. Pryke, "The Identity of the Qumran Sect: A Reconsideration," *Novum Testmentum* (1968): 43–61; and Pére R. De Vaux, "Essenes or Zealots?" (review article on G.R. Driver's *The Judean Scrolls*), *New Testament Studies* (1966–67): 89–104. Whatever problems Qumran may present in its later development, Zealotism and Apocalypticism may be seen as fairly consistent expressions of "temporalized" and "spiritualized" religion at the time of Jesus' earthly ministry.

5. On the meaning of the kingdom, see esp., Ladd, *Presence,* and Ladd, *Theology,* pp. 45–134. For a discussion of the history of interpretation of the kingdom, see Norman Perrin, *The Kingdom of God in the Teachings of Jesus* (Philadelphia: Westminster Press, 1963), esp. pp. 13–157; and the lengthy introduction to the new edition of Johannes Weiss, *Jesus' Proclamation of the Kingdom of God,* trans., ed., intro. by Richard Hyde Hiers and David Larrimore Holland (Philadelphia: Fortress Press, 1971), pp. 1–54.

6. Cf. Mark 1:14,15; Matt. 4:12,17.

7. Perrin, *Kingdom of God,* p. 175.

8. E.g., Brandon, *Jesus and the Zealots,* and Robert Eisler, *The Messiah Jesus and John the Baptist,* trans. A.H. Krappe (New York: Dial Press, 1931).

9. Cullman, *Jesus and the Revolutionaries,* pp. 8f.

10. See further, Matt. 13:39,40,49; Luke 20:34f; Matt. 24:3; John 18:36.

11. Hans Küng, *Justification,* trans. Thomas Collins, et al. (New York: Thomas Nelson, 1964), p. 209. See also James Buchanan, *The Doctrine of Justification* (London: The Banner of Truth Trust, 1961), pp. 240ff.

12. M. Meimertz, *Theologie des Neuen Testamentes,* vol. II (Bonn, 1950), p. 115f; cited in Küng, *Justification,* p. 209.

13. Cf. Rom. 3:22; 4; 5:1,2; 9:31,32; Gal. 2:16; 3:11; 3:25,26; Eph. 2:8; Phil. 3:9; etc.

14. Cf. Rom. 3:27,28; 4; 11:6; Gal. 3:10,11; Eph. 2:9; etc.

15. See G.C. Berkouwer, *Faith and Justification,* trans. Lewis B. Smedes (Grand Rapids: Eerdmans, 1972), p. 137.

16. James Buchanan, *The Doctrine of Justification,* cited in Carl F.H. Henry, ed., *Basic Christian Doctrines* (New York: Holt, Rinehart, and Winston, 1962), p. 214.

17. For the discussion that follows, cf. Berkouwer, *Faith and Justification,* pp. 129–40, esp. pp. 135–37.

18. Ibid., p. 137.

19. Henry, ed., *Basic Christian Doctrines,* p. 228.

20. Though the word "cooperation" is used here intentionally, it is not used in a sense that would suggest any kind of synergism in which God and man "pull on the same rope." Cf. Donald G. Bloesch, *The Christian Life and Salvation* (Grand Rapids: Eerdmans, 1967), pp. 28, 128–29. Similarly in *Justification* (see p. 265) Küng argues that Trent did not teach synergism.

21. Cf. Bloesch, *Christian Life and Salvation,* pp. 85ff.

22. Verse 23 reads further, "provided that you continue in faith . . ." This would seem to suggest that it is possible not to continue in faith, or in other words to fall away from faith or to fall out of grace (see also, e.g., Gal. 5:4; Heb. 4:6; 1 Tim. 1:19; 2 Pet. 2:20,21). However, we may wish to interpret such passages, they certainly need to be taken with the utmost seriousness. Even if one concludes that we can never "lose our salvation" it would seem from passages such as these that where one does not "continue in faith" and where faith is not expressed in "works of love" such faith may be a pious illusion and

therefore not saving faith. Cf. Bloesch, *Christian Life and Salvation*, pp. 89f.

23. Francis Oakley, *The Medieval Experience* (New York: Scribners, 1974), p. 146. Professor Oakley provides in this work a highly creative interpretation of the church's significance in shaping medieval life and also in shaping the modern consciousness.

24. Ibid., p. 163.

25. Cf. Rodoslav A. Tsanoff, *The Great Philosophers*, 2nd ed. (New York: Harper and Row, 1964), p. 194.

26. Cf. Lane T. Dennis, *A Reason for Hope* (Old Tappan, N.J.: Fleming H. Revell, 1976), pp. 100–06 and 115–53.

27. Cf. Ibid., pp. 83–99.

28. Küng, *Justification*, p. 250.

29. *Ibid.*, p. 250. Küng argues further in this chapter entitled "Sola Fide" (pp. 249–63) that Trent and Reformation theology—if understood properly—are in complete harmony.

30. Even the Plymouth Brethren, who claim to have no ecclesiastical structure, have developed a number of "quasi-structures," such as missionary societies, mission boards, financial institutions, etc. Similarly, in the sense described here, the Plymouth Brethren would be very sacramental in view of the fact that they place a high value upon Baptism and the Lord's Supper, celebrating the latter on a weekly basis in a simple, moving service.

31. Or in more conventional Catholic language, "grace is mediated through the sacraments," because of God's real and active presence in and through them, as perceived in faith.

7. A Call to Sacramental Integrity

by

THOMAS HOWARD

Thomas Howard is Professor of English at Gordon College in Wenham, Massachusetts. He earned the Ph.D. at New York University and is author of a number of books including Splendor In The Ordinary *(Wheaton: Tyndale House, 1976).*

We decry the poverty of sacramental understanding among evangelicals. This is largely due to the loss of our continuity with the teaching of many of the Fathers and Reformers and results in the deterioration of sacramental life in our churches. Also, the failure to appreciate the sacramental nature of God's activity in the world often leads us to disregard the sacredness of daily living.

Therefore we call evangelicals to awaken to the sacramental implications of creation and incarnation. For in these doctrines the historic church has affirmed that God's activity is manifested in a material way. We need to recognize that the grace of God is mediated through faith by the operation of the Holy Spirit in a

118

*notable way in the sacraments of baptism and the Lord's Supper.
Here the church proclaims, celebrates and participates in the
death and resurrection of Christ in such a way as to nourish her
members throughout their lives in anticipation of the consummation of the kingdom. Also, we should remember our biblical designation as "living epistles," for here the sacramental character of
the Christian's daily life is expressed.*

The Cleavage in Christendom

The notion of sacrament has not been a lively one in evangelical Protestant imagination over the centuries since the Reformation. The historical reasons for this are clear enough: It was
the great burden of the Reformers to take the mysteries of the
faith that had, in the late Middle Ages especially, been almost
entirely located for popular imagination in external forms
such as masses, pilgrimages, shrines, sacred objects, and so
forth, and to plant these mysteries once more in the place
insisted upon by the prophets and apostles as the only proper
locale for them, namely, the heart of man.

A drastic and clean sweep, surely, was necessary. The faith
is, precisely, a matter of *faith*, and this is a matter of the heart. It
will do you no good to trek to Santiago de Compostella, or to
the shrine of Blessed Thomas at Canterbury, nay, or even to
the Holy Sepulchre itself. What is needed is a pilgrimage of the
heart, from unrighteousness to purity. Again, your money and
your beads will have not the slightest effect on your soul's
account (and you may be sure there is no tally being kept in any
such place as Purgatory). What is needed is repentance, which
means only one thing in the gospel, namely, a turning away
from sin and the pursuit of holiness from your heart. This
alone will put you in the way of salvation. And yet again,
nothing at all is achieved by your simply being under the roof
where a Latin mass is being said. What is needed is not miracles
of chemistry up there on the stone slab, full as it is of dead
relics, but rather the miracle whereby your own heart becomes
the altar on which sacrifices of righteousness are offered in

faith to God. All these external acts and objects, far from being helpful, are positively destructive. They nullify the very evangel of grace itself.

The cleavage between these two ways of perceiving how the mysteries of the faith are to be applied to the soul of man was a stark and abysmal one, and for almost half a millennium now it has remained a great gulf fixed, at least in popular Christian imagination. In the last thirty years, of course, the theologians and liturgiologists and ecumenical emissaries have, in the course of their painstaking work, discovered that it is not a gulf that cannot be bridged; indeed, they have constructed the anchor-work and pinnings for very long spans to be thrown across this gulf, it appears. And ordinary lay Christians on both edges of the chasm have been startled, especially in services where the various "charisms" are manifest, to discover fellow-believers and brothers among those whom they had been taught were their worst enemies. But five hundred years' worth of rhetoric, suspicion, and even bloodshed (alas for the Marian martyrs and the Elizabethan martyrs, and for the Revocation of the Edict of Nantes, and Piedmont, and for Irish martyrs on both sides)—five hundred years of this cannot be wafted away in one or two or three decades of good will.

But, of course, it is not all mere hot-headedness, ignorance, and prejudice. It is not just zealots and partisans who keep enmities, or at least vastly differing views, alive. Even the most patient, wise, and saintly soul can see that a simple matter like whether to put your pulpit or your altar at the center of focus is no mere stubborn bit of social custom. It is a question that reaches all the way to the root, not only of the Christian apprehension of the gospel, but of human imagination itself. Given strongly-held presuppositions, it becomes almost a matter you will fight over. (Nay, it *has* been fought over: Many a church has been pillaged, defaced, or bombed for just such a reason.)

But to repeat, it is not just the zealots and partisans who cannot get beyond the difference in vision at stake here. Sage and holy souls on both sides of the question are able to articulate, with inexpugnable lucidity and consistency, just why they see things the way they do. Is the bread up there Christ's body or is it not? Yes. No. Well. . . . Is it salutary for my soul that I hear the promise of Christ's forgiveness made audible through the larynx of another mortal man, or is it confusion? Yes. No. Well. . . . Is the gospel adequately guarded and enshrined forever in the pages of the Bible, or is Scripture itself entrusted to the church, which is Christ's presence on earth? Yes. No. Well . . . .

The differing answers to these questions are held with intelligence and devotion by the best and most scholarly minds in Christendom. They are not mere red flags.

So that we cannot, in issuing a "call" to evangelical imagination, simply assert that View A is orthodox and View B thereby heterodox. Our task here is to try to describe, in the least possible inflammatory way, just how it comes about, for example, that Christians who believe utterly the Epistle to the Hebrews, with its insistence on one priesthood and one altar in the heavenlies, nonetheless seem to have a multitudinous priesthood and innumerable altars here on earth. The difficult point for evangelical imagination to grasp here is that this view is held, not by a Christendom that rejects the Epistle, but by one which passionately espouses its teaching.

What Is Sacrament?

To come, then, to the question from which all these differences arise. It might be variously phrased. What is sacrament? What is sacramentalism? Is it necessary? Inevitable? Optional? Is it mere frill? Does it represent a muddling and adulterating of the pure gospel of faith? Is evangelical Protestantism the richer or the poorer for having preached a religion virtually devoid of any reference to sacrament as such? Is Catholic Christendom unfaithful to the gospel by having decked the dominical and apostolic teaching with sacramentalism? Perhaps the best place to begin on an answer is to attempt a definition of sorts.

Sacramentalism may be understood as the Christian view that sees the physical as potentially the vehicle of the spiritual. A sacrament, in this view, is both what it appears superficially to be—Ritz crackers, say—and also a mode under which something beyond the ingredients in those crackers is made real and present to us. For a sacramentalist, then, a sacrament is more than a souvenir or a memento, helping to jog his memory with a picture of something. The physical components of the sacrament (the bread, or the wine, or the water) stand, as it were, on the interface between what we can see and what we can't. They do, of course, remind us of something that we are trying to recall and witness to; but beyond this helpful function, they make that something real to us, in a mystery.

In a mystery: Here is, perhaps, the key. There are no propositions that can quite compass the transaction that occurs in sacrament. Here we are brought up to that frontier where propositions tend to get muddled and die away. No one—no father, doctor, or council—has ever found precisely the adequate phraseology and vocabulary to exactly define what is going on in the sacraments.

Here, perhaps, lies one great difficulty that evangelical imagination finds with the notion of sacrament: Protestantism (and with it, then, evangelicalism) is strongly propositionalist, from its doctrine of Scripture right on through to its practice of theology and preaching, to its piety that is characterized by such verbal exercises as Bible study and testimony. The notion that the greatest mysteries of the faith will never quiet yield themselves to our efforts to articulate them, while of course affirmed by Protestant imagination, nevertheless finds itself at times crowded into a corner in the great effort to articulate Christian vision in satisfactory propositions.

It is not that the sacramentalist is antipropositional. A sacrament makes no sense if there is no idea proposed as to what is going on. It becomes mere talisman, or mumbo-jumbo (which it had become for many by the sixteenth century). Orthodoxy can never be maintained by waving wands and thuribles about. Somewhere in there an Athanasius or an Augustine needs to pick up his pen and spell out what is wrong with the wrong view, and why it is that the right view alone is to be held by everyone. But having granted this, any Christian knows that on every single point of the faith we come eventually to the place where we must say, "It is a mystery. I cannot press my explanation any further than this." Creation, Fall, Redemption—who is equal to these topics?

It makes sense, then, that at the very center of our activity as the church, we find actions that involve us visibly and unmistakably with the mystery of the gospel, namely, Baptism and the Eucharist, commanded by the Lord and obeyed ceaselessly ever since. How merely physical stuff can have this focal and exalted place in Christian vision stumps us. It is an absurdity. But then, we recall, "merely physical stuff" has exactly this focal and exalted place in every single one of the great events of the faith, and this is what the sacramentalist seizes upon. Look at these events: Creation, Fall, Redemption, Incarnation, Passion, Resurrection, Ascension, Pentecost, and Eucharist. Is there one of them that occurred in a purely "spiritual" realm? The whole drama was played out, to the confusion and outrage of all gnostics, Manichaeans, and rationalists of all time, in starkly, embarrassingly physical terms. He *made* something (water and rock and whales) and everything praised Him; we men botched it by making a grab for it and trying to call it our own, and everything fell into corruptibility; He planned a rescue and a restoration, and chose a man and a tribe and demanded lamb's blood; then He took on this flesh Himself; in the suffering of that flesh He effected the redemption of the world; that Flesh came out of the grave, the sign and guarantee to all heaven and hell that victory was won; that Flesh ascended into the midmost mysteries of the triune Godhead; the Godhead came down on the tongues and into the flesh of men and women; and, for them, at the center, for as long as history would go on, bread and wine.

The whole scheme was carried forward in heavily carnal terms. Unlike the deities of rationalists and Eastern seers who beckon us all away from the world of water and soil and flesh and blood and bread and wine into the aether of bodilessness, this God returns us to it and it to us in something infinitely richer than escape. It is Redemption. The gathering together of all things (all spirits, and all flesh) in Christ, says the apostle. Nothing to be swept under the rug.

How, then, is this vision of things to be mediated to us and kept alive in us? Through propositions? Yes, propositions: the Proverbs, the Sermon on the Mount, the apostolic preaching and writing. So far so good. And through what else? Through commandment, where the truth takes on the form, this time not of mere proposition but rather of edict—Get up and help your neighbor get his ox out of the ditch—with its corollary: That is one way into an understanding of what the truth is. And through history, where truth takes the form now, not of mere proposition, but rather of narrative—The God whose name is Yahweh has done this and this and that for you; remember it—with its corollary: That is one way into an understanding of what the truth is. And through Psalm, where truth now takes the form, not of mere proposition but rather of poetry and dance—*Benedicite, omnia opera domini!* Praise him on lute and cymbal!—with its corollary: That is one way into an understanding of what the truth is. And through prophecy, where truth takes the form, not of mere proposition, but rather of dazzling imagery—Ephraim is a cake not turned; I saw a woman clothed in the sun; dragons and horsemen and falling towers—with its corollary: That is one way into an understanding of what the truth is. And through parable, where truth takes the form, not of mere proposition, but rather of vignette—Once upon a time there was a woman mopping her floors—with its corollary: That is one way into an understanding of what the truth is. And supremely, through enactment, where truth takes the form, not of mere proposition but rather of the Word become flesh.

One Whole Fabric

Sacramentalism may be understood then, as the view that sees a discernible meeting point in appointed physical vehicles between the visible and the invisible realms. Put it another way: Sacramentalism rejects sheer dualism, if by this we understand that the universe is forever divided utterly between the temporal and the eternal, or the material and the spiritual, or the visible and the invisible realms. It rejects this much of popular Platonism, that "reality" is located wholly in the spiritual realm, and that the material world is illusion. Hence, it rejects also many of the popularly held teachings of various Eastern religions that speak of an escape *to* reality *away* from the visible world.

Indeed, a true sacramentalism would be unhappy with continual references to the "visible" and "invisible" realms as though they were two different worlds, even though it is aware that this distinction is helpful for our human patterns of thought. For at the foundation of sacramental vision lies the robust affirmation of the whole creation, from seraphim to clams to basalt, as *one good fabric.* There are not two entirely distinct worlds in the creation, the visible and the invisible. God is the maker of heaven and earth, in one great creative action. He made spirits and he made stones, and they all inhabit one huge world. It is evil that has introduced the distinction and the enmity. It is after the Fall that you get the corruptible and the incorruptible realms being distinguished. And here especially it must be remembered that corruption applies as much to the spiritual realm as to the material. The devils and damned souls in hell are, precisely, spirits in a state of corruption. Just as good food rots, and silver tarnishes, and our flesh sickens and decays, all of it because of evil, so the lordliest celestial spirits may rot and tarnish and decay into fiends in hell. It is the same process, the same fabric.

So that a sacramentalist would suspect that our inability to live in one, undivided realm of creation is perhaps one of the disabilities brought upon us by our own sin. Indeed, although there is not a syllable explaining this in the Bible, and certainly no scientific research will ever be able to uncover any data on the point, it may be imagined that a film as it were, was imposed on our very eyeballs at the Fall, so that we lost the ability to perceive the one whole fabric in which angels and ourselves inhabit a continuous realm. We can no longer *see* very much. We had sown a disjuncture into things by our action (this is ours, and that is God's), and we reaped the harvest in our very eyeballs. We had now to perceive things as divided. Who knows?

But in any event, proceeding from the doctrine of Creation as it does, sacramentalism would affirm the oneness of the whole creation, and it would see the material world (that is, as much of the whole fabric as we can descry with our eyes and our senses) as both real and metaphorical. The material world is understood to be real and not illusory for the reasons just now touched upon. We come now to this world perceived as metaphorical.

The World as Metaphor

This means that, besides being simply itself, as a sort of dead end, the material world also presents reality to our mortal eyes in a mode suited to these eyes, namely in visible shapes and textures and colors. It is always signalling to us, so to speak. It is perhaps like a messenger or a herald: The herald is not less a man, or less himself, by virtue of being charged with the duty of announcing someone else. He is a man who is a herald. Similarly, the visible creation has this duty, on the sacramentalist view. In its forms and colors, which are beautiful in themselves like the bright tabard of the herald, it speaks to us of that which is beyond itself. Indeed, just as the brightness of the herald's tabard derives its colors and design directly from the arms of the king whose emissary the herald is, so the material creation exhibits the pattern of that which is beyond it.

Another way of putting this, of course, is to say that anyone who cares to look—any god, angel, or human—will see played out in the forms and colors and substance of this world *that which* is true on all levels in the universe, visible or invisible, from God on down. It is not as though this visible world has had an extra job assigned to it of play-acting the truth just for us mortal men to behold, besides getting on with whatever else it is naturally designed to do. Rather, it is that in this very natural design of it we find the only pattern there is, exhibited and enacted under the particular modality of visible matter.

For example, we see in this world seeds sown in prepared soil in springtime, and then nothing happening, and then shoot, then stalk, then flower, fruit, and harvest. Well, that is the natural design of things in this world; but it also happens to be a bright metaphor, in the sense that right there, in terms of seed and soil and sunlight, we see enacted *that which* is true at the top and bottom of everything, namely that life proceeds from death, and that only by something's falling into the ground and dying can we ever, in any realm, expect a crop. What is true agriculturally is also true in the highest realm ("... he suffered and was buried . . ."), and in every realm in between.

We can see it in politics, for example: In order for a state to function at all and reap the "harvest" of order and peace, the various interest groups that inhabit the state must compromise their special interests, and this compromising is a small form of dying, is it not, in that one has to lay one's own case, or part of it, into the ground in order that the crop of peace in the commonwealth may appear. It is visible all through the political fabric, right down to local routines like stop signs and traffic lights (my right to move ahead is "buried" for a moment so that your right may be exercised). Order is the crop proceeding from the sowing of all these little deaths.

And we see the same principle again in the emotional and psychological realms. A child who has been allowed to believe that everything is his for the demanding grows up testy, querulous, and rapacious. We saw this in the generation in the late nineteen-sixties who, never having been told by their parents that time, labor, and patience is the price exacted by life for all really worthy things, supposed that by screaming and raging and sitting down on their campuses, they could change the whole order of things and get what they wanted. They knew nothing of corns of wheat falling into the ground and dying and lying silent and dead, perhaps for decades or centuries. No one had ever showed them Flanders Field or Arnhem, where tens of thousands of mortal seeds lie in silence while the rest of us reap the harvest of whatever peace issued from those sowings. On the other hand, the truly free child is the one who has learned that satisfaction will forever elude the one who grabs, but will come, strangely, to the one who has learned to "bury" his self-interest in that odd exchange called sharing. This, of course, is the whole principle of love, which is at the root and pinnacle of everything. Laid-down life. Bliss from self-giving. Harvest from planted seeds. Life from death.

The point here is that all this which is true politically and psychologically and theologically we may see played out for us any time we care to look at a potato field or a pot of geraniums. No other principle has been at work. The physical world furnishes us with endless metaphors, not by our poking about and extracting occult significances from things, but simply by our observing what is perfectly and plainly going on.

So, the sacramentalist (or, surely, any Christian, or indeed any person who cares to look) sees material things as bodying forth their own excellence and beauty, and at the same time bespeaking significances beyond themselves. The plumage of finches and tanagers—does it not present to us a small case in point of what glory is—*all* glory? The massif of Mont Blanc— may we not fetch thence some small inkling of God our Rock? The sound of running water, of a winter wren, or indeed of flutes—do we not in these hear intimations of a greater music spoken of in Psalm and apocalypse? The sacramentalist would suppose so.

This, then, is the starting point for sacramentalist vision. The visible and proximate may be, indeed is, "full of the majesty of Thy glory." Things are excellent in themselves and excellent in their heraldic office. The scheme seems to run all up and down the fabric, so that when we find it isolated and pressed into special service at the center of the Christian mysteries, in the Eucharistic feast, we are not scandalized. What did we suppose bread and wine were about in the first place?

Sacramentalism Vs. Pantheism

A note of demurral and caution may be sounded here. A true sacramental vision differs utterly from the diffuse and pantheistic aspirings of the romantic poets who thought everything was divine. Sacramentalism, while keenly aware of the metaphorical, or heraldic, office of material things, rigorously reserves the specific *sacramental* function to the occasions when these things are set aside for that function by the clear and ordered intention of the church. Traditional Catholic, Orthodox sacramentalism would differ wholly, then, from the Quaker view, for example, which eliminates special sacramental observances in worship since *all* eating and drinking are held to be "sacramental." There is a blurring here, the sacramentalist would reply. It is true that all eating and drinking proceed upon the same principle as the sacrament, namely life laid down that others might be nourished; but the Lord did something separate, conscious, significant, and special, on the first Maundy Thursday evening at the Supper, and the church has always understood that act to have constituted her Lord's example and charge to her to *focus,* in specific acts of worship, what is of course generally true anyway. It would be analogous to the lambs brought to the Tabernacle in the Old Testament: *Of course* every lamb ever born belonged to God; but it is necessary *for us* that this diffuse truth be focused and enacted by a conscious, costly, physical betokening. A general affirmation of the truth does not seem to be enough.

A Crux

Here, indeed, there would be a crux between nonsacramentalists and sacramentalists. The former would hold that it is enough to believe the truth in faith since the locale of true religion is in the heart. The latter would hold that, because we are not pure spirits, we mortal men must also *enact* that inner belief in specific, material terms. The giving of alms, for example: It is not enough to say to the pauper, "Depart, be warmed and fed." Or the giving of a kiss to our beloved: It is not enough to insist that they *believe* that we love them. Or the conscious setting aside of this loaf and this cup from among thousands of loaves and cups. We need to have what we affirm physically vouchsafed to us. We are not disembodied spirits—mere intellects and wills. We have lips and tongues and stomachs, and these are not despised nor huddled into a corner in the scheme of Redemption. This bread and this wine has been given to us. Angels, presumably, do not require it just this way; but we mortals do.

Sacrament as Enactment

Which brings us to a further principle at work in sacramentalist vision. Besides seeing the material world as both real and metaphorical, sacramentalism would see the principle of *enactment*, or ceremony, to be very much of the essence. And here again, a sacramentalist would urge that he is not fetching some occult or arcane notion from afar and imposing it on things. Rather, he would insist, he is merely proceeding upon plain principles that are there for anyone to see.

The principle of enactment, then, which is certainly at work in Baptism and the Eucharist, is when we "act out" what we believe to be true. If we will reflect for a moment, we will see that not only are we not doing something peculiar here, but we are rather carrying to its ultimate point of significance a phenomenon that is absolutely central to universal human practice.

This phenomenon is visible in every tribe, culture, and civilization from the beginning of myth and history right on down to the present. It is this: We mortal men are ritual creatures. We are forever "acting out" things.

Take greetings, for example: There is hardly a culture anywhere that does not have some ritual convention for greeting people. It may be a handshake, a bow, a nod, or whatever, but the principle is always there. We act out with physical gestures (grasping hands; bending the waist; nodding) something that is invisibly at work in the situation. We wish to signal the ideas of welcome and peace and friendship, so, rather than going through a long discourse on the idea, we do something physical. We are ritual creatures. We take the significance, and let a conventional, physical ritual carry it.

Similarly with eating. The business of eating is nothing more, at least on a pragmatic view, than the transfer of energy from point A (the peapod, or the rasher of bacon) to point B (my bloodstream) so that I can keep going. The progress of technology has devised enormously efficient means for streamlining this transfer (bottles of glucose, tubes, liquid protein, and needles): But no tribe or society has adopted these streamlined methods for lunch or dinner. Why not? Why do we all follow the laborious and circuitous route of fixing and cooking and garnishing? To say nothing of setting tables with napkins folded thus, and cutlery (silver cutlery, even) arranged thus, and china and crystal set out thus. Or, short of that, paper napkins and plain crockery on the kitchen table for breakfast.

It is because we are ritual creatures. These routine functions somehow seem to us to imply more than mere utility. To try to bespeak our sense of this further significance in things, we deck them. We festoon them. We set them about with ritual, even if the ritual is nothing more than folding a paper napkin or holding the door open for a lady. Physical things and acts carrying great burdens of significance.

Any religious person is familiar, of course, with this sort of thing. Many Christians, for example, bow their heads to say grace, or kneel down to say their prayers, or lower their voices in church buildings. What is this all about? Is it not once more our human way of registering in a physical way (neck or knee or voice box) some significance that seems to be there and that we want to acknowledge?

Now it is worth noting that when we mortal men come up to the great, intractable mysteries of human life (birth, sex, and death), we ritualize our responses to them, too. It is not simply breakfast, or saying hello that we deck. Each one of these big events represents "nothing more" than a biological event, and a very routine one at that. Nothing unusual. And yet all of us, Hottentots and Saxons, Slavs and Polynesians, New Yorkers or Samoans, deck these events elaborately. We ritualize our responses to them.

Birth, for example. In our own culture the decking tends to run along white, yellow, pink, and blue lines, with bows, ruffles, silver spoons, and pretty blankets being the tokens. Horses don't bother with this, and yet they have the same experience biologically, foaling away merrily just as we do. What is the trouble with us that we add all this extra? Clearly we are creatures such that the mere obstetrics of the event will not entirely cover the topic for us. Something has happened, and we must do something beautiful about it, something beyond the forceps and thermometers and diapers and charts. Those are the accoutrements of obstetrics and pediatrics; but these bows and frills and christenings we concoct are the index of something even deeper in our humanity.

And sex. The approach of a man to a woman is again "simply" a biological event, and a timeworn one at that. Nothing unusual. But all of us, Hottentots and Saxons and the lot, set this approach about with very high hedges (at least we did; the present Western experiment in "free" sexual congress arises from time to time in history, and nothing lasting is ever built on it). We festoon it all solemnly. Whether this festooning takes the form of puberty dances or shared milkshakes or taboos, leading up to a feast or a nuptial mass in Chartres, the phenomenon is the same, namely, the marking by ritual tokens the significance in the event.

And, of course, death. When we have filled in our medical reports and have made our sociological analyses of the dynamics of dying and have staved off corruption with embalming fluid and copper vaults, we set it all about with long palls, drawn hearses, and sung requiems (or whatever). We *do* something about these events, and that something is inevitably ritual.

The Paradox of Play

There is an odd paradox here (and one that appears important to sacramentalist vision), namely, that when we come to the most serious events of all in human existence, we find that we have somehow moved beyond all of our techniques and measures and methods, and that we must in fact *play*. For that is what ritual, or ceremony, really is. It is a form of play-acting. We are doing what children do with their doll houses and toy trucks; we are saying, "Let this represent that." With the children it is, "Let this doll represent Mummy or Queen Eleanor," or "This Dinky Toy is my Mack truck." With the adults it is "Let this gowned procession represent the bride's approach to her lord," or, "Let this rite bespeak our honor to the dead person."

Ceremony, ritual, enactment: "These forms of "play" touch on the sources of what we human creatures are.

But there is more. A sacramentalist would suspect that all this ritualizing and decking is not simply a question of us men taking inert data (birth, sex, death, or anything else that human existence is made up of) and festooning them all arbitrarily, thereby expressing some interior, purely fanciful feelings on our part about these data—feelings that have no connection with external reality. Quite the contrary. He would urge that the ritualizing with which we deck these events (the processions, the cakes, the place mats) is the quintessentially human mode of perceiving and marking the truth about these events. The events are not being forced by us into some Procrustean bed of ritual: Rather, human imagination perceives something real, and something that the eyes of clams or horses can't perceive. It sees a pattern of significance, a web, so to speak, binding together all the diffuse data of the world and of our experience; and, by setting these data in a formal context of ritual, ceremony, and enactment, it attempts, not to impose an arbitrary and fanciful pattern *on* the data, but rather to elicit, in obedience to what is there, this marvellous interconnectedness among things.

The Doctrine of Correspondence

It is from this deeply human awareness of pattern and inter-connectedness among things that everything that marks human life as human arises. All poetry, all music, all courtesy, all architecture, all grace and ceremony and costume—everything, in a word, that distinguishes our life from that of chimpanzees. It is, of course, the principle of metaphor that is at work here once more. B may symbolize A for us, not because we reach wildly about and seize B arbitrarily, but rather because there is at work in B this much of what we perceive to be also at work in A.

We perceive, for example, not an arbitrary but an *appropriate* connection between high ceilings and kings. Why? Because in both there is a notion of exaltedness. The high ceiling answers to this high prince. We fashion something in realm B (architecture) that both answers to and enhances what we see in realm A (politics). Does it falsify things? No, we would say: If someone urges that tunnels and crawling are specially appropriate to kings, then we and all the whole race of man would have to reply that if this is so, we will need to erase everything and start all over again, recasting the entire known universe.

The same would be true for all such correspondences. Unless we are prepared to jettison everything we know of man, God, and the world, and call all our perceptions into doubt the way some philosophers reject the validity of rational thought thereby ending the philosophical process—unless we are prepared to do this—we must proceed along the lines that seem to be here around us, and that are answered to by everything that we know, including, for Christians, revelation itself. Gold and not offal is the right metaphor for glory; white and not black is the right metaphor for purity; peak and not slough is the right metaphor for joy; eagle and not pterodactyl is the right metaphor for splendor; lamb and not crocodile is right for innocence.

Two observations about metaphor (and hence about sacrament) ought to be made at this point. First, we may find two very different images for a single truth we are trying to come at; but this does not controvert the point being made here, namely that there must be some "real" connection between the two terms in the metaphor. For example, we may speak of Christ as king or servant. Is that a confusion? Or does it mean that any metaphor will do?

Neither. In the first place we find that the notion of Christ is such that the metaphor "king" will catch *thus much* about him, but that the metaphor "servant" catches this other that is also true about Him. His kingship, for example, is not to be compared to that of Nebuchadnezzar or Ghengis Khan except in its absoluteness and splendor. We want to introduce the further notion of servant at some point in order to get the whole picture right. Again, we may speak of Him as lion and lamb, priest and victim, husband and brother. Is it all a jumble, forcing us to the conclusion that any metaphor will then do?

No. In the second place, we may not speak of Christ as thug, or as snake, or as butcher. Those would do violence to the idea in question. Now it may be observed here that, while the word "thug" implies evil in itself, and hence is wholly inappropriate, and obviously so, the words "snake" and "butcher" are not like this. There is nothing wrong with snakes and butchers. Snakes are part of the creation, and must lead their lives and obey their natures, just as field mice and chickadees do. Likewise butchers: Many of them are saints and heroes. But we may not speak of *Christ* as snake or butcher, not because of any inherent flaw in these two creatures, but rather because the thing that becomes operative in the metaphor arouses a confusion. It would ask more of us than may be asked if we pictured Christ as a snake, even if we do grant that snakes are a lovely part of creation, since snakes glide along on their bellies, and there is nothing about Christ that is clarified for our imaginations by such a picture. Similarly the butcher: We may speak of both Christ and that butcher as *men*, or as workmen, or as husbands, etc. But we don't speak of Christ as butcher since the word implies slaughter and chopping and shedding blood, and that is not part of Christ's office. The butcher's office is good and praiseworthy, but it does not furnish us with a useful, or indeed a possible, picture of Christ's office.

The second observation that ought to be made here is that it is preeminently via the metaphorical mode, so to speak, that this "interconnectedness" among things may be perceived. It is difficult to satisfy us by other means—by logic, for example, or chemistry. To be sure, a syllogism can display for us the process whereby we move from, say, lamb to Christ: Lambs look and act harmless; Christ (at least in his sacrificial role) looked and acted harmless; therefore lambs and Christ are to that extent similar. So far so good. But that leaves the data inert, so to speak. We don't hang syllogisms on the wall, or hail them in epic and carol. Our humanity wants to paint, with Van Eyck, the Adoration of the Mystic Lamb, or wants to sing, "At the Lamb's High Feast We Sing." (Now in so far as there is a kind of religion that says we ought *not* to follow Van Eyck, or sing, and that we ought to restrict our apprehension of these things to verbal propositions, then the sacramentalist would admittedly belong to a very different outlook. The effort being pursued in this essay is to persuade those who may doubt it that sacramentalism is "nothing more" than the gathering of our whole humanity into joyous obedience to what nature and the gospel both ring out to us always and everywhere.)

Logic, then. It teaches us, and it certainly harmonizes with what we see metaphorically, but it does not entirely compass the business for us. Similarly with chemistry. The straight chemical designation for Gold (Au), or the position of gold in the periodic table of atoms, with its valence and so forth, does not very readily yield data useful to us in deciding that gold is an appropriate metaphor for glory, as opposed, say, to zinc. We can't wring from chemistry any easily visible connection between gold and glory. Zinc is as legitimate and secure a part of the table as is gold. It would be difficult to insist on gold's special place as metaphor by means of what we can establish by this method. (Who is to say that it is not possible, though: The periodic table itself may be a thrilling cryptogram, bursting and sagging with data all rushing straight to the Te Deum. But once more, we mortals are creatures such that, sooner or later we want to lift the gold off the chart and make a crown out of it; if we have been wrong and foolish to have done so, then we shall have to erase everything and begin over again.)

The point being urged here is that the faculty that perceives the appropriateness of one thing serving as a metaphor for another is the human imagination. The metaphor is presented to imagination, and assented to by imagination. And something true seems to have been articulated.

It becomes clear at this point that imagination, far from being a matter of foolishness and the conjuring up of what can't possibly be true, is the mode of perception that may lie closest to the truth of our humanness. Angels and seraphim don't *need* imagination presumably, since it is said that they behold Reality directly; and animals don't *have* imagination as far as we can tell; but we humans perceive Reality, unlike angels, mediated through a thousand oblique angles and colors in the prism of creation, and we forever try, unlike animals, to descry a pattern by relating all the angles and colors to each other.

For the sacramentalist, this is all enormously important. It is to this sort of creature—to us—that the sacraments have been presented. Our Lord did not call them sacraments, of course; that is our name for them. But he commanded water, and bread and wine; not for angels, and not for the beasts, but for us men.

Internal and External

There may, no doubt, appear to be an anomaly here. The whole point of the gospel was that external observances now be planted in the heart, and that what had hitherto been a matter of physical gestures and material tokens now move beyond that superficial level into the inner man. A sacrificial spirit now, not just a pennyworth of alms. Purity of heart, not just ceremonial washing. Real justice, not merely Sabbath observance. Faith first and faith last. If this is so, then how can our Lord have tied things down once more to material objects? Why did he not insist that the whole locale of his gospel be in the heart? Or rather, since he did insist on this, why did he then blur it by introducing these few external things?

Three Responses

There have been, since the sixteenth century, three responses in Christendom to this apparent crux. On the one hand would be the view that the water of Baptism and the bread and wine of the Eucharist are to be understood entirely spiritually and hence that Christians need not include in their piety or church order any special sacramental observances. Faith, not Baptism, is what saves us. The communion of the heart, not of bread and wine, is what nourishes us. Hence we will dispense with any such observances at all. There are a few groups (the Quakers and the Salvation Army, among others) that espouse this view.

At one step from this would be the view that these physical tokens, while proper, even necessary, since they were commanded by the Lord, have no significance beyond that of underscoring, as it were, what is real and true enough without them. Baptism for example, does not *do* anything for a person other than declare to all and sundry what has already been effected by grace and grasped by faith. No real transaction occurs. This is a widespread view in Reformed churches.

On the other hand is the view commonly called sacramentalism, in which, in a mystery, something real does occur with the application of the water of Baptism, and with the partaking of the bread and wine. The line between this and the former view is not necessarily to be drawn along the Protestant-Catholic frontier, since the Reformers themselves were fiercely divided over exactly how we should understand what is going on. Calvin taught what might be called a high view of sacrament; Luther and Zwingli quarrelled bitterly over the point at Marburg; and the sixteenth-century Anglicans held all manner of views, themselves changing over the decades of turmoil. So, we are not speaking here of simple sectarian lines.

The Efficacy of Sacraments

The questions are rife, of course. The commonest fear about sacramentalism from the nonsacramentalists is contained in the phrase *ex opere operato,* the fear here being that it may be believed that the sacraments are magic, having some automatic and inevitable efficacy all by themselves, and that a person can be saved, for example, by being plunged into water, or can imbibe a bit of grace automatically by eating a wafer, wholly apart from any question of faith ever entering in. Although this is, unhappily, a widely held view among poorly taught Christians in sacramentalist churches, it is not the true teaching of sacramentalism. A sacramentalism that teaches any doctrine other than the Pauline doctrine of salvation by grace through faith is heterodox. A sacramentalist would see the "efficacy" of the sacraments to be hinted at in the analogy of sunlight: Sunlight is "in itself" strong and health-giving and efficacious, but of course we can shut it out by drawing the blinds. The sunlight must be "received" by us, so to speak, for it to do its work in us. Similarly (and any analogy for a mystery like this is full of flaws), the sacraments will not work magically on us, penetrating any carapace of sin or unbelief we have around us. They are strong and efficacious to do their work, but it is on the living hearts of human beings that they work, not on stocks and stones. We *can* nullify them if we will, just as we can grow pallid and wan by refusing the strong light of the sun.

The problems come when we try to understand exactly the sense in which the sacraments operate. And obviously this essay will not settle what Fathers, councils, doctors, Reformers, and Anabaptists have not been able to settle to everyone's satisfaction. It must be strongly urged, however, that a robust sacramentalism in no way calls in question the Pauline doctrine of salvation by grace through faith. The sacramentalist would try to explain, in answer to a question on this point, that it is the same Lord who charged His apostle with the gospel of grace who also commanded water, and bread and wine—physical transactions—apparently central enough to the mysteries of the gospel that they be reiterated as command both by the Lord and by His apostles. Preach and baptize. That is how men are to be saved. Do this in remembrance of Me, and when you do, I will give My very Body and Blood to you.

The sacramentalist would not be prepared to "spiritualize" these commands and promises. Just as all the mysteries of revelation and redemption have been mediated to us in starkly physical terms, so these. It is not for nothing that the gospel unfolds itself this way. We may not be able to compass it intellectually, but then which of the mysteries can we thus compass? The Lord's commands and promises are not idle nor arbitrary, surely: He did not merely cast about for some handy and helpful reminder of the mysteries and light upon water, and bread, and wine. Surely (says the sacramentalist) these tokens themselves stand on that interface between what we can see and what we cannot, specified and hallowed by the Lord Himself.

We run the risk of trivializing our Lord's express commands if we relegate them to a purely ancillary, even peripheral, place in our church order and teaching. The mystery of regeneration, presented to us in baptism—have we quite understood why the Lord insisted on this physical rite? And the great Eucharistic mysteries, in which common stuff that we bring is received and given back to us, according to the Lord's promise, as his Body and Blood—surely this is no peripheral thing? We have here the great paradigms of the gospel, given to us and enjoined upon us, flesh and blood creatures that we are, by the Word Incarnate.

Summary

The foregoing observations might be summed up thus: In the sacraments of the church we find focused, articulated, set forth, and mediated to us, in obedience to the Lord's example and command, the great mysteries of Creation, Fall, and Redemption. The Creation is one holy fabric. Our sin has rent and despoiled it, making things "secular." In the sacraments we find things returned to their rightful use and place, that is to say, redeemed. (In Eden no special baptism or eucharist was necessary, presumably, since nothing needed to be refocused, never having been blurred. No special setting apart of things for God—no "hallowing"—needed to occur since we still had the clarity of vision that saw truly, and saw that everything was God's. We saw perfectly clearly that all was gift, and hence we offered all back in the oblation of thanksgiving. No washing was needed since all was pure. No blood was asked since nothing needed ransoming. Now it is different.)

Further, in the sacraments, the church proceeds upon three great principles that are manifestly woven into the texture of the Creation and of our humanness. First, the material world is metaphorical. That is, it speaks of the oneness and wholeness of Creation in the visible, plastic terms that our mortality can grasp (we having forfeited our ability to experience this seamlessness). Second, enactment lies very close to the root of our peculiar humanness. That is, we mortal creatures come at reality ceremonially. (And, lest it be feared, we are not speaking particularly of "High Mass" here: A paper napkin folded on the breakfast table, or a Saltine and paper cup of wine—these are all we need for our rituals.) And, third, it is this very enacting that elicits a real, not a fanciful, connection between things. It is a specially clear mode of perception. Things come at us in a blur and a tumble generally, and in the sacraments things are focused and set in harmonious order; not just water, or bread and wine; but our whole existence. We enact our Redemption here.

For the modern evangelical churches in the West, it may be part of the Lord's answer to their prayers for renewal, that they consider most earnestly, just what the Lord was doing in giving us these rites that we call sacraments. Does evangelical piety, teaching, and church order really stand in the deepest, richest, and most ancient stream of Christian vision, or does it represent, in this area at least, an unwitting strangling of some of the flow?

Postscript

Four comments may be added here, which do not necessarily form part of the main argument.

1. It will have been noted that the whole foregoing argument lies outside the threshold of liturgical studies. That is, there is no description of the liturgy itself. The reason for this is obvious and twofold. First, it is too vast a topic for a brief essay. Second, it would have been the wrong place here to have begun suggesting how various church groups are to give shape to renewed sacramental awareness. The author's own point of view would place him deep within the stream of ancient Catholic orthodoxy; but one who holds this view must remember that all liturgical studies are in a state of vast upheaval now.

2. For a sacramentalist, church history is enormously important. The gospel is not disembodied. The Holy Ghost did not cease operation among us thirty years after Pentecost. It is of the most lively interest to a sacramentalist just how the emerging church gave shape to its understanding of the gospel. After all, these were the people who had been taught by the apostles. For this reason, the writings of the Fathers, especially the early ones like Ignatius of Antioch, Polycarp of Smyrna, and Clement of Rome, are seized upon with great curiosity by sacramentalists. Authority is attached to these writings—not, of course, an authority even approaching the apostolic; but nonetheless, an authority such as one would give to venerable and wise teachers. We are not the first Christians, in other words, to have opened the pages of the New Testament. How did our forerunners, especially those closest in to the apostles, handle it? What did they do? This matters.

3. A comment heard sometimes concerning sacramentalism is that it looks pagan. All the bowings and processings and smoke and vestments that seem to attend it all—is this not just what the heathen do? Yes, says the sacramentalist; it is exactly what the heathen do, and they do it because it is what human beings do. We—all of us—are creatures who want to adore. And we want to bring all of our gifts to the shrine. We want to

deck the important things beautifully. If we bring our adoration and our offerings to the wrong shrine (as Christians would think pagans are doing) then the trouble is not with the adoring or the offering, but rather with the *object* of this worship. You ought to be bringing your offerings to Yahweh, not to Baal.

Of course, all the patently grotesque, immoral, and cruel practices associated with heathen shrines are purged away in Christian worship. The smoke of incense at Christian altars does not hide licentiousness and murder; rather it ascends with prayers and praises coming from the hearts of the Christians gathered there. (If it does, in fact, hide licentiousness and murder, as might be the case in places where Christian rite is not purified and animated by real obedience to the gospel, then the situation is analogous to the filthy offering of Hebrew sacrifices so excoriated by the Old Testament prophets, and needs to be denounced.)

Any Christian, furthermore, no matter how stark and unadorned his church order, must admit that he is doing what heathen do. If he so much as bows his head to pray—nay, if he so much as *prays*—he is at that point doing what heathen do (as opposed to secularists, who pray to no one). The Christian would have to answer simply, "Yes, I am like the animist in that I *pray;* but I think he is addressing his prayers to a god who is not the living God of heaven, who alone ought to be addressed."

4. There is a difficult point of "liturgical *time*" that might help to undo an apparently Gordian knot for nonsacramentalists. To them, it looks as though having priests and altars represents a failure to grasp the teaching of the book of *Hebrews* that there is only one priesthood and one altar. The Sacrifice was offered once for all, two thousand years *ago*. The endless ceremonial obligations of the Law were swept away. No further propitiation is necessary.

Two things need to be said here. On the one hand, a notion that has filtered down to hordes of Christians from clerical sacramentalism for some hundreds of years now, especially in the West, is that the priest up there at the altar is, in fact, offering endless sacrifices, and that there is some astronomical numerical tally being kept, so that the more sacrifices you can be present at, the better off you will be. God, remote and angry, must be repeatedly propitiated. These Christians live for their whole lives without ever once hearing effectively the teaching of the Book of Hebrews (or any of the other Epistles for that matter). If something like this has been true in the Roman Church, it is the Romans themselves who are now aware of it. It may take generations to get the truly "evangelical" note of apostolic preaching sounded throughout the vast provinces of that church, but then it is not we who hold the divine stop watch.

On the other hand, the true teaching of Catholic sacramentalism has always been that there is indeed only one Priest and one altar, and that the priests and altars that we see in churches here below are the visible means by which the church, as the Body of Christ the High Priest, actively and perpetually participates in His self-oblation that occurred in our history, to be sure, at one point in the past, but which oblation is an eternal fact. He is always the Lamb slain from the foundation of the world; He is always the Priest; He always intercedes for us. And we, His priestly people, participate perpetually in this activity. Priests are the ones appointed in the order of the church here on earth to "preside" (the early church spoke of the officiant at the Eucharist as the "president") at the occasions when the whole company of gathered people representing Christ's body offer up with Him the only Sacrifice there is or has ever been. It is a question of the church—Christ's body—being one with Christ the Head in His ministry. And further, that ministry is perpetual, not in the temporal, sequential sense of being repeated endlessly century after century, but rather of its being an eternal, and hence daily real and present fact, always to be enacted, always to be marked, always to be participated in. Jewish altars looked "forward" in time to the only Sacrifice there ever was; the Christian altar looks "backward" only in the sense that the only Sacrifice there ever has been or ever will be was made on the stage of our history at a real point many years ago. Something *was* finished in Judaea, under the hand of Pontius Pilate the governor; but nobody knows exactly how to speak about this mysterious relationship of eternal fact to temporal event except to say that the events were real and unique and irrevocable. (Palestinian geography will be named, presumably, in the songs of the saints in heaven long "after" our time and our universe have been folded up like a scroll.) In the Eucharistic liturgy, the church ·declares and enacts, in physical terms, her natural citizenship in the Eternal City. She breaks through the veil of mere temporality, so that there is no question of there being many priests and many sacrifices.

The evangelical churches might, conceivably, be one of the instruments God could use in helping His whole church return to an authentically *gospel* sacramentalism that embraces, proclaims, and enacts as it should its part in the great mysteries of redemption.

8. A Call to Spirituality

by

DONALD BLOESCH

Donald Bloesch is Professor of Theology at the University of Dubuque Theological Seminary, Dubuque, Iowa. He holds the Ph.D. degree from the University of Chicago and is the author of numerous books including Jesus Is Victor! Karl Barth's Doctrine of Salvation *(Nashville: Abingdon Press, 1976) and* Essentials of Evangelical Theology *(New York: Harper & Row, 1978).*

We suffer from a neglect of authentic spirituality on the one hand, and an excess of undisciplined spirituality on the other hand. We have too often pursued a superhuman religiosity rather than the biblical model of a true humanity released from bondage to sin and renewed by the Holy Spirit.

Therefore we call for a spirituality which grasps by faith the full content of Christ's redemptive work: freedom from the guilt and power of sin, and newness of life through the indwelling and outpouring of his Spirit. We affirm the centrality of the preaching of the Word of God as a primary means by which his Spirit works to renew the church in its corporate life as well as in the individual

*lives of believers. A true spirituality will call for identification
with the suffering of the world as well as the cultivation of
personal piety.*

*We need to rediscover the devotional resources of the whole
church, including the evangelical traditions of Pietism and
Puritanism. We call for an exploration of devotional practice in
all traditions within the church in order to deepen our relationship
both with Christ and with other Christians. Among these resources
are such spiritual disciplines as prayer, meditation, silence, fasting, Bible study and spiritual diaries.*

The Problem in Spirituality

The word "spirituality" is not often found in traditional
evangelical vocabulary, but it is roughly equivalent to what
evangelicals have meant by "piety" and "devotion." Spirituality
must not be taken to mean simply the spiritual side of man's
life, as in a dualistic asceticism. In the biblical or evangelical
sense, spirituality refers to the life of the whole person in
relationship to the Spirit of God. It concerns the vertical relation between man and God but as it impinges on the horizontal
relationship between man and his neighbor. Spirituality is the
life of man in the light of his faith in God. It has to do not just
with Christian doctrine but with the practice of the Christian
life. Its meaning is not simply service and stewardship but a
devotion and commitment to the living God that is lived out in
daily life.

The problem in modern evangelicalism, and indeed in the
modern church as a whole, is a dearth of spirituality on the one
hand and a misguided spirituality on the other. The former
can be seen in a dead orthodoxy that makes doctrine rather
than life and experience the pivotal center of Christian faith. It
is also to be detected in a liberal social activism that reduces
religion to ethics and loses sight of the transcendent dimension
altogether. Misguided spirituality is noticeable in the aesthetic
ritualism of high-churchism, the hyperenthusiasm of some
charismatics, and the legalism and moralism that dominate

many of the sect groups. This is not to deny that the wind of the Spirit is indeed discernible in the religious renaissance today, including the charismatic renewal, the liturgical movement, and the upsurge in religious community life. Yet true spirituality is not uniformly present in any of these movements, and the causes can be traced partly to a neglect of sound doctrine stemming from a superficial knowledge of the Bible and a wholly inadequate understanding of the evangelical and catholic tradition of the church. The Spirit of God is either grieved by manipulative revival techniques or quenched by a stultifying formalism and ritualism.

Current spirituality within both Protestantism and Catholicism is for the most part incurably anthropocentric. The concern is with the fulfillment and well-being of the self rather than the glory of God and the advancement of His kingdom. This anthropocentric or egocentric religiosity is prevalent not only in evangelical circles but also in liberal and neo-Catholic circles. Religion is either confused with sociological goals or reduced to psychological states. The faith of the holy Catholic church is obfuscated by an unhealthy introspection and groupism. A theology of interpersonal relations and spiritual experiences has supplanted a theology of the Word of God.

Hallmarks of Evangelical Spirituality

The word "evangelical" is here being used primarily in its theological rather than its popular sense and consequently includes the authentic biblical piety that has now and again appeared in Catholic and Eastern Orthodox churches as well as Protestant. At the same time it should be acknowledged that evangelical piety in its best sense was realized to a high degree in the Reformation of the sixteenth century as well as in those spiritual movements of purification subsequent to the Reformation: Pietism and Puritanism. The Catholic movement of Jansenism (associated with Pascal) also exemplifies some of the salient emphases of historical evangelicalism.

Certainly one of the prime distinctives of evangelical spirituality is *soli Deo Gloria,* glory to God alone. Because God is sovereign and holy, all the glory must be directed to Him and not to the creature, even to the church. To give glory to God does not mean quietism but active obedience and service to our neighbor. Calvin put it this way:

> We are not our own: in so far as we can, let us therefore forget ourselves and all that is ours. Conversely, we are God's: let us therefore live for him and die for him. We are God's: let all the parts of our life accordingly strive toward him as our only lawful goal.[1]

Not only Calvin but Augustine, Luther, Loyola, Edwards, and many other famed theologians of the church universal have accentuated this motif in the Christian life. To be sure, sometimes the emphasis on the glory of God has been contrasted with a concern for personal salvation so that the latter is seen as something unworthy of the Christian. There is scriptural basis for arguing that it is precisely when we are concerned for our personal salvation and for the salvation of others that God is glorified and that His kingdom is advanced. The orthodox Reformed theologian A. Polanus of Basel affirmed a double goal in theology: the glorification of God and man's attainment of eternal salvation. Philip Spener also reflected this biblical balance when he declared: "Next to God's glory my great object is that God shall save my soul and those whom he has entrusted to me."[2] And as the church Father Irenaeus so poignantly put it: "The glory of God is man fully alive."[3]

This is not to deny, however, that God's glory takes precedence over desire for personal salvation and spiritual security. We should be concerned for our salvation for the sake of God's glory and not for our own sake. Likewise we should be active in the service of the needy in order to glorify God and advance His kingdom. A catholic evangelical spirituality is radically but not exclusively theocentric, since it also includes a concern for God's creatures who are made in His image.

Again, evangelical spirituality is marked by an acknowledgement of the divine authority and primacy of Holy Scripture as the written Word of God. It is regrettably true that many evangelicals in the past as well as the present have entertained a Docetic view of Scripture that unwittingly denies its real humanity and historicity. We tend to forget that the Bible is the Word of God in and through the words of men who lived in particular cultures and periods of history and whose language mirrors this historical background. Evangelical theology insists upon the paradox that the Bible is the revelation of God in the form of human witness. Yet in and through this human witness can be heard God's own self-witness, but this hearing is dependent on the interior witness and illumination of the Holy Spirit. Evangelicals treasure the Bible not as a past historical record, but as the reservoir and conduit of divine truth (Carl Henry)—as the earthen vessel through which the Spirit of God speaks to us today.

Evangelical spirituality insists on the primacy of Scripture over the church and religious experience, though at the same time it recognizes that the Bible is spiritually effective only in the context of the community of believers and only where its message is personally appropriated in the experience of faith. The primacy of Scripture is a thoroughly catholic as well as evangelical doctrine as George Tavard has reminded us in his *Holy Writ or Holy Church*.[4] Augustine voiced the views of many of the church fathers: "Who does not know that the Holy canonical Scripture is contained within definite limits and that it has precedence over all letters of subsequent bishops, so that it is altogether impossible to doubt or question the truth or adequacy of what is written in it?"[5] Scripture is the infallible norm by which the church measures its dogmatic formulations through the ages. The Holy Spirit interprets the Scripture to the church, and the church in turn, illumined by the Spirit, interprets this truth to its people and to the world at large.

Certainly the radical sinfulness of man also figures prominently in any assessment of evangelical spirituality. Our Reformed forefathers used the controversial term "total depravity," and the meaning is not that there is no remnant of goodness within man, but rather that he is totally unable to believe or come to God by his own power. Both Augustine and Luther referred to the "bondage of the will" whereby man is enslaved to the power of sin and can be redeemed only by the initiative of God in bestowing His unmerited grace. Evangelical piety also speaks of the continuing sinfulness of the Christian, and this means that the entire Christian life must be one of repentance (Luther). This is not to deny the reality of divine sanctification in the life of the believer, but it is a process that never fully eradicates the proclivity to sin. Consequently the evangelical Christian feels called to repent of his virtues as well as his vices, since even his good acts always proceed from less than perfect motivations.

Closely related to the sinfulness of man is the stress on the sovereignty of God's grace. Salvation by grace (*sola gratia*) was not only a major theme of the Reformation, but it was a cardinal doctrine of Ambrose, Augustine, and Aquinas as well—and indeed was formally endorsed by the Second Council of Orange (529). Apart from grace we are dead in our sins (Eph. 2:1,2). Our salvation, therefore, rests not on our own merits or works, but instead solely upon God's undeserved mercy and favor revealed and fulfilled in Jesus Christ. Man is justified while still in his sins (Luther), but the gift of justification is accompanied by the inward renewal of the Holy Spirit so that he is not only outwardly pronounced righteous but inwardly cleansed. This evangelical orientation is to be contrasted with every form of Pelagianism and semi-Pelagianism that holds that man in and of himself can do something to procure his own salvation.

This brings us to the atoning work of Christ on the cross, which is the pivotal center of evangelical devotion. Evangelicals see Jesus Christ as our substitute and sin-bearer before they see him as example and model. The atonement is both a satisfaction of God's holiness and an expiation of man's guilt; it is also an incursion of triumphant divine love into history. It is both vicarious suffering in the place of man and vicarious identification with the plight of man. In the Protestant Reformers as well as more recently in Karl Barth the triumphalist motif (or classic theory) and the satisfactionist motif (Latin theory) have been brought together in an enduring and creative synthesis.

What is the implication of the substitutionary atonement for the Christian life? It means that the Christian no longer needs to suffer retribution because of his misdeeds, since his guilt and sin have been borne by God Himself in the form of man. The Christian no longer suffers penalties for sin, but he still endures disciplines and trials from the hand of God that strengthen him in the daily battle with sin, death, and the devil. Spirituality is a response to a salvation already achieved; it is not the means by which we win pardon and approval from God. It is a demonstration of our gratefulness for a finished salvation (Heidelberg Catechism, Question 86) as well as the vehicle by which the fruits of Christ's salvation are applied to our lives by the Holy Spirit. Our spirituality is a sign and parable of the perfect salvation of Christ as well as a testimony to the interior work of the Holy Spirit who makes this salvation efficacious in our lives. We cannot atone for the sins we or others have committed (this has been taken care of by Christ), but we can bear witness to His atonement through steadfast and costly discipleship.

The outpouring of the Holy Spirit is indeed another cardinal theme of evangelical piety. Bishop J. C. Ryle, an evangelical Anglican, spoke for many when he said: "We need the work of the Holy Spirit as well as the work of Christ; we need renewal of the heart as well as the atoning blood; we need to be sanctified as well as to be justified."[6] Apart from the gift of the Spirit we would remain spiritually lost and condemned. But because the Spirit enters our lives we are brought into living contact with the atoning work of Christ and are thereby united with Christ in His passion and resurrection. Evangelical spirituality speaks of this first entrance of the Spirit into our lives as the new birth. Baptism with water is insufficient for salvation: We must be baptized with the Holy Spirit as well if we are to know the new life in Christ (cf. John 3:5; Acts. 8:16,17; 19:1–7).

The cruciality of preaching as the primary means of grace is also enunciated in evangelical spirituality. It was St. Paul who proclaimed: "Faith comes from what is heard, and what is heard comes by the preaching of Christ" (Rom. 10:17). John Calvin explained: "God . . . deigns to consecrate to himself the mouths and tongues of men in order that his voice may resound in them."[7] And in the words of P. T. Forsyth: "With preaching Christianity stands or falls because it is the declaration of a Gospel. Nay more—far more—it is the Gospel prolonging and declaring itself."[8] In authentic Reformation theology the preaching of the gospel is regarded as the Word of God just as much as Scripture itself, though there is admittedly a certain dependence of the first on the second, since it is the Scriptures that furnish the basic content of our preaching.

As the Pietists rightly remind us, in the selection as well as the proclamation of the Scripture text, the ambassador of Christ must be open to both the illumination of the Spirit and the guidance of the church, but the former must always take precedence. The bane of much so-called orthodox preaching is that the Spirit is quenched and grieved, and consequently the sermon takes the form of a dull recitation of historical truth rather than a biblically inspired message that conveys the "power of God unto salvation" (Rom. 1:16, KJV).

It is abundantly clear that the stress in traditional evangelical piety is on the audible over the visual, since faith comes primarily by what is heard and not by what is seen. This accounts not only for the prominent role of preaching but also for the place for public prayer and the singing of hymns in the life of faith. At the same time, authentic evangelical spirituality does not exclude the visual as a medium of continuing revelation. It is not only the Bible proclaimed, but also the Bible read that promotes faith and devotion to Christ.

Moreover, the visible Word, the sacraments of Baptism and the Lord's Supper, are deemed highly important in both the reception of faith and continuation in the faith. The sacraments are to be understood, however, not as rites that work automatically by virtue of simply being performed (*ex opere operato*), but as rites that receive their efficacy through being united with the Word of the gospel and the faith of the participant, a faith that is given by the Holy Spirit.

Not only the preaching of the Word but the sacraments are to be seen as veritable means of grace, outward signs by which divine grace is communicated and implanted in the believer. A false sacramentalism, which is detrimental to true faith, must not blind us to the abiding value of the sacraments when conjoined with the Word.

The call to a spirituality that is genuinely evangelical and biblical will also include a rediscovery of the theology and practice of prayer. While fully acknowledging the substantial contributions of the tradition of Christian mysticism, we cannot readily adapt the biblical model of prayer to the mystical one, which is heavily influenced by Platonism and Neoplatonism. The heart of biblical prayer is the pouring out of the soul before God (cf. Ps. 142:2; Isa. 26:16; Heb. 5:7), supplication and intercession on behalf of the oppressed and afflicted.

Biblical Christians cannot agree with Meister Eckhart who when asked to pray for someone replied: "Why not be your true self and reach into your own treasure? For the whole truth is just as much in you as in me."[9] For Eckhart intercession is not necessary because every person possesses within his own soul the divine spark that needs only to be fanned into a living flame. In biblical, evangelical theology, on the other hand, humanity is spiritually lost apart from Christ, and even the new humanity is a frail reed that survives in a darkened world only through its union with Christ. Intercession is the heart of the fellowship of the church apart from which the spiritual life of each of its members cannot long endure.

Prayer to be sure takes other forms besides supplication and intercession. There is adoration and praise, which the mystics remind us is the height and goal of all true prayer. There is also thanksgiving and the confession of sins, which are integral to biblical prayer (cf. Ps. 32, Isa. 6). Yet it can be shown that the element of petition is present in all these other forms. We must ask God to accept our sacrifices of praise and thanksgiving as well as hear our confessions. Even the one who prays the prayer of adoration enters the presence of God as a suppliant.

Meditation is to be regarded not as a higher form of prayer than petition but as a supplement to true prayer. It can also be viewed as a preparation for prayer. Luther frequently recommended the salutary practice of meditation on the passion of Christ as an aid in spiritual growth. Prayer is a dialog that entails listening as well as speaking, but to seek to transcend the dialogic element in prayer through contemplation of the mysteries of God is foreign to the biblical understanding of prayer and devotion.

Again, the eschatological hope plays a significant role in all piety that claims to be biblical and evangelical. This hope is not wholly otherworldly but also this-worldly in that it perceives that some of God's promises will be realized on earth as well as in heaven. This millennial dimension of the Christian hope has often been misrepresented in literalistic terms, but it is nonetheless true that this dimension formed a part of the spirituality of many of the church fathers as well as of the founders and leaders of evangelical Pietism and Puritanism.[10] Karl Barth has remarked that biblical Christianity must always contain an element of chiliasm,[11] though this element must forever remain in the background and not the foreground of Christian thinking.

The Christian hope gives assurance to the Christian as he struggles to maintain the faith and grow in the faith. He is aware not only of the victory of Christ on the cross and the present indwelling of the Spirit but also of the future victory whereby the kingdoms of this world will be transformed into the kingdom of God (Rev. 11:15). He realizes that though the devil is still the titular prince of this world, his power has been taken from him in the Cross and Resurrection victory of Christ and that he is now waging a battle that has already been lost. Yet the public revelation and consummation of the victory of Christ has still to take place, and this is why the Christian can live a life of confidence, though not of recklessness, in the certain knowledge that the future belongs to God. The church should be on the offensive, not the defensive, in the warfare against the powers of darkness; this is implied when Christ promises that "the gates of hell shall not prevail" against his church (Matt. 16:18, KJV).

As can be seen, evangelical theology and piety contain a moral dualism that depicts the world as a battleground between the forces of good and the forces of evil. The reality of a demonic adversary to God and man is keenly perceived in this kind of orientation. A dualistic mentality is conspicuous in Augustine's *City of God,* in Luther's *Bondage of the Will,* and in Calvin's *Institutes of the Christian Religion.* It is certainly also very much present among the church fathers including Irenaeus, Tertullian, Origen, and Gregory of Nyssa, all of whom upheld what has come to be called the classic theory of the atonement, which, sees the atoning work of Christ as a victory over the demonic powers of darkness. This moral dualism has been eclipsed in modernistic theology beginning with the Enlightenment of the eighteenth century, and it has been muted in the neo-orthodoxy of Karl Barth and the neo-Catholicism of Karl Rahner, which tend toward a monism of grace.

Finally, we need to give attention to the truth that authentic spirituality will be a holiness that is not removed from the travail of the world, but one that is lived out in the midst of it. Max Weber and Ernst Troeltsch have referred to the life-style of the Reformation and post-Reformation churches as an "inner-worldly asceticism" since it involved the subduing of the powers of chaos within society as one lived out his vocation in the world. Its purpose was the advancement of the kingdom of God in the world, not a flight from the world into a purely spiritualized kingdom. Ascetic disciplines were seen not as means of salvation but as aids in pursuing the Christian life in the stations of life to which God has assigned us. This is not to say that there can be no place for withdrawal in authentic biblical piety, but withdrawal must always be related to return. The purpose of withdrawal should be a more radical penetration into the citadels of the world. Religious orders and communities have a place in the evangelical vision, but only if they serve the great commission—if not through preaching—then through prayer and deeds of mercy.

Spirituality is indeed a life lived out in the world sustained by faith in the transcendent God. Once this transcendent dimension is ignored or downplayed, as in current liberalism, then spirituality is converted into ethics, and faith becomes confused with love. Karl Barth has given this timely word of warning: "Clever enough is the paradox that the service of God is or must become the service of man; but that is not the same as saying that our precipitate service of man, even when it is undertaken in the name of the purest love, becomes by that happy fact the service of God."[12] Secular and liberation theologies err when they practically equate humanitarian service and social reform with kingdom service, though they must always be seen as integrally related.

Need for Catholic Continuity

Evangelicalism needs to rediscover its roots not only in the piety of the Reformation and the great revivals, but also in the great Catholic heritage of the church. It can be shown that Roman Catholic mysticism played a formative role in Martin Luther's spirituality, though he broke with mysticism in his concept of forensic justification.[13] Not only the sixteenth century of the Reformers was a significant period for great preaching but also the fourth and early part of the fifth centuries that included John Chrysostom and Augustine. Other Catholic saints and mystics who were noted biblical preachers were Bernard of Clairvaux and Savanorola. At the same time it can be shown that many of these men were far more preoccupied with the law of God than with the free gift of salvation through the atoning sacrifice of Christ.

Certain Catholic practices of devotion that had faded into the background in the days of the Reformation reappeared in Pietism and Puritanism, though these practices were now given an evangelical foundation. Among these were the spiritual disciplines of meditation, silence, fasting, retreats, and spiritual diaries. In addition the Pietists emphasized lay Bible study, prayer lists for intercession, and hymn sings, all of which were not conspicuous in later medieval spirituality. Any of these disciplines can become a new law, but rightly understood they can also be a powerful means for strengthening the life of devotion.

In seeking continuity with the tradition of the whole church, one must be ready to judge every theory and practice in the light of the gospel. Traditions can become obstacles to spiritual growth as well as aids, and they need to be measured in the light of God's self-revelation in Holy Scripture. At the same time we believe that the Spirit of God is at work in the church as well as in the Bible, and that the Spirit interprets to the church the intended meaning of the Scriptures. We reject the idea of new revelation, but we can affirm continuing revelation in the sense of an illumination of what has already been revealed.

In assessing the relationship of the Bible to the church, we affirm the written Word as the judge and creator of the church, and the church as the servant of the Word. It is nevertheless true that it is in the church that the Bible becomes alive, and only through the agency of the church is the message of the Bible conveyed to the world. Christ is the living voice, the Bible is the Word that He speaks, and the church is the mouth through which He speaks. The Spirit interprets the Word to the church, and the church in turn interprets the Word to the world. The church attests and proclaims this Word, but it does not authorize or authenticate it.

The Bible is not chronologically prior to the church if the church is meant to include the community of Israel (as Calvin understood it), but the message of the Bible, the Word of God, is ontologically prior to the church, since this Word resides within God Himself. Protestants must not claim that the Bible is simply imposed upon the community of faith and does not arise from within the community through the work of the Holy Spirit. At the same time our Catholic brethren must recognize again, as did many of the fathers and doctors of the church, that the ultimate origin of the Bible is transcendent, beyond history, though the actual writing and transmission of the sacred manuscripts took place within history.

Again as evangelicals we can affirm the Catholic doctrine of a special ministry of the Word, but this holds true only in the context of the priesthood of believers. The ministry of the Word and sacraments is a special office within the church, but this does not exclude other offices and ministries, such as evangelism, healing, prophecy, pastoral care, etc. Nor does it imply that the continuity of the church rests upon an apostolic succession conveyed through the sacramental laying on of hands by the apostles to their successors and continuing through the history of the church. The real apostolic succession is one of continuity with apostolic doctrine and faithfulness in carrying out the apostolic charge.[14] Those who receive the special call from God to the ministry of the Word and who fulfill their vocation by upholding the apostolic faith as declared in the New Testament are the bona fide successors of the apostles. We here agree with Hans Küng that all the members of the church in the exercise of their special charisms and ministries stand in the succession of the apostles so long as their witness concurs with that of the New Testament.[15]

In our dialog with Catholic and Eastern Orthodox Christians, we also need to acknowledge the sacraments as veritable means of grace but only in relationship to and in dependence on the proclaimed Word of God. The sacraments derive their efficacy not from the rite in and by itself, but from the rite united with the Word of God. With regard to the Lord's Supper, Küng perceptively remarks: "The elements by themselves have no significance . . . it is in the light of the word that we should understand the Lord's Supper. The word here has not primarily the function of consecrating and transforming, but of proclaiming and testifying."[16] A catholic evangelical spirituality will be sacramental: It will affirm the reality of the redeeming activity of Christ in the rite of Baptism and the Eucharist. Yet it will not be sacramentalistic or sacerdotalistic, since the Word of God remains central, and the priesthood of the Lord is shared by every believer.

This brings us to the truth that the emphasis in evangelical piety is on the inward over the outward. Jesus told his disciples to pray in secret and not to exhibit their piety before others, as did the Pharisees (Matt. 6:5,6). He also warned them that they should be oblivious to their good deeds (Matt. 6:3,4), since true spirituality is focused on pleasing God, not ourselves. At the same time we will ignore another significant dimension of our faith if we make piety exclusively inward. Its basis and origin are inward, but it must give rise to good works in both the personal and social sense. It must also be expressed in a religious cultus that includes sacramental rites, since ritual properly motivated is an authentic expression of piety. Piety needs to be incarnate in outward forms and practices if it is to maintain continuity with the faith of the church, though its essence lies in the new birth and the indwelling of the Spirit which are invisible, intangible, and impalpable (Luther).

An evangelical catholic spirituality will include both the theology of glory (evident in the so-called Romantic mystics) and the theology of the Cross (which was Luther's emphasis). The Christian life should be seen as both a constant battle against the powers of darkness and a joyous walking in the light of Jesus Christ. It involves both daily repentance under the Cross and an experience of the glory that is yet to come. Christians now have "the first fruits" of the Spirit (Rom. 8:23), but in the eschatological future they will be transformed by the Spirit into the likeness of Jesus Christ.

In the kind of spirituality we uphold, evangelism is the central thrust of the church's mission, but evangelism is inseparably tied to social service *(diakonia)*. Our task in life is both the heralding of the gospel of salvation and following this gospel in self-giving service to others. Social service may sometimes have chronological priority over evangelism in that on occasion we must meet the physical and emotional needs of our hearers before we can announce the good news to them. Evangelism has theological priority, however, since the deepest need of our fellowman is salvation from the bondage of sin and life with God in eternity.

A catholic evangelical spirituality is characterized not by a flight to the past (as in Gallicanism and some forms of Anglo-Catholicism) but instead by a breakthrough into the future. As catholics we need to conserve the abiding values of the church tradition, but as those who appeal to the biblical prophets, we also need to be open to the present and future illuminations of the Spirit as He guides us into a ministry relevant to today's and tomorrow's world. We need to reform our structures and rephrase our doctrine in the light of the Word of God, which addresses us now in the concrete situation in which we find ourselves. We should have an earnest respect but not a nostalgia for the past since God calls us to live and act in the age and culture in which He places us. Evangelicals should not imitate Catholic or Eastern Orthodox practices of devotion but instead endeavor to learn from these heritages, and such learning involves critical examination as well as spiritual discernment.

Again true spirituality will strive to overcome the world rather than flee from it (as in the dualistic asceticism that characterized much of medieval piety). It will seek not an ascent to divinity beyond life in the flesh (as in Neoplatonism and Gnosticism) but a recovery of true humanity as this is seen in Jesus Christ. Yet the liberation from sin that the gospel accomplishes does not give us permission to satisfy the lusts of the flesh. In the battle that we are called to wage in the world we need to be properly trained, and this entails a restraint on our sinful inclinations. Bonhoeffer put it very succinctly: "If there is no element of asceticism in our lives, if we give free rein to the desires of the flesh . . . we shall find it hard to train for the service of Christ."[17]

In seeking to maintain continuity with the catholic tradition and recover certain devotional practices of the pre-Reformation church, we must guard against the danger of reducing spirituality to a law or technique. We would then again be in the camp of legalism, the very peril Paul warned against in his letter to the Galatians. At the same time we must bear in mind that spirituality is not only a gift but also a task. We are called to strive for the holiness apart from which no one will see the

Lord (Heb. 12:14), and this means a life of unceasing struggle and prayer.

In rediscovering our theological and historical roots, we must not be content with finding the marks of the church only in the scriptural preaching of the gospel and the right administration of the sacraments (as in the Reformation). Apostolicity and catholicity are also to be found in following in the steps of the apostolic ministry as well as in heralding the apostolic message. The fellowship of love *(koinonia),* which is concerned with the imitation of Jesus Christ as well as the gift of His grace, is still another reliable mark of the true church, an emphasis found at least implicitly in Pietism. Certainly we must include the urgency of mission as one of the marks of the true or spiritual church, and this too characterized the renewal movements of Pietism and Puritanism. The classical attributes of the church (oneness, holiness, apostolicity, catholicity) are all reflected and attested in the practical signs of gospel preaching, sacramental observance, fellowship, and mission.

Pathways to Evangelical-Catholic Unity

There are both right and wrong ways to forge a catholic, evangelical theology and piety. One wrong way is that of re-pristination by which we seek to restore practices and devotions in the past simply because they have the force of tradition behind them. This concern is conspicuous in Edward Pusey and the Oxford Movement that succeeded in instilling new life into the Anglican church, but at the cost of losing sight of the hard-won doctrine of justification by the imputed righteousness of Christ. Moreover, the preaching of the gospel was relegated to the background as the blessed sacrament became the focal point of worship.[18] This is not to minimize the religious earnestness and genuine desire for Christian unity that distinguished this renewal movement. Nor is it to overlook the new social consciousness that it created within Anglicanism.

Another less than satisfactory direction was taken by Nikolai Frederik Severin Grundtvig (1783–1872), Danish Lutheran theologian, who subordinated the Bible to the church. In his view the gospel was spread by the living power of the apostles and the church independent of the written word. The living Word, which is prior to the written word, is given to each successive generation in the two sacraments. Emphasizing growth in faith over conversion, he saw tradition, not Scripture, as the basis for doctrine and practice.

Among luminaries in the past who better approximate an authentic catholic evangelicalism are Count Ludwig von Zinzendorf; Wilhelm Löhe, German Lutheran theologian and founder of the Neuendettelsau deaconess house; John Nevin and Philip Schaff of the German Reformed church in America; P. T. Forsyth; and Nathan Söderblom. All these men affirmed the primacy of Scripture and the central doctrines of the Reformation, though they all sought to make a prominent place for regeneration and sanctification as well as justification. This is not to deny that traces of Romanticism were present in some of these men. Certainly we should also look to the Reformers, Luther and Calvin, as persons who tried to uphold an evangelicalism rooted in Scripture while maintaining continuity with the tradition of the church universal.

Tragically, the reforming impulse that they inspired was rejected by the Catholic church, and Christian unity was irreparably sundered. At the same time we should remember that their goal was not to found new churches but to purify and reform the church of their fathers. In so doing they were sometimes led to discard more in the Catholic tradition than was warranted by Scriptural principles, but nonetheless their intention was to revitalize the historic church. An authentic evangelical catholic spirituality will seek not to bypass the Reformation but to go through and beyond it, since that movement recovered biblical doctrines that lie at the very heart of the Christian faith.

Forsyth put his finger on the essence of a catholic evangelical spirituality when he declared: "Christianity is not the sacrifice we make, but the sacrifice we trust; not the victory we win, but the victory we inherit. That is the evangelical principle."[19]

Would that we might recover this kind of spirituality in our churches today.

Notes

1. John Calvin, *Institutes of the Christian Religion* III, 7, 1, ed. John T. McNeill, trans. Ford L. Battles (Philadelphia: Westminster Press, 1960), p. 690.

2. Marie E. Richard, *Philip Jacob Spener and His Work* (Philadelphia: Lutheran Publication Society, 1897), p. 46.

3. Irenaeus, *Against Heresies* IV, 20, 7.

4. George Tavard, *Holy Writ or Holy Church* (New York: Harper & Bros., 1959).

5. Cited in ibid., p. 16.

6. J.C. Ryle, *Holiness* (Cambridge: James Clarke, 1956), p. 23.

7. Calvin, *Institutes of the Christian Religion,* IV, 1, 5, p. 1018.

8. P.T. Forsyth, *Positive Preaching and the Modern Mind,* 4th impression (London: Independent Press, 1953), p. 3.

9. Raymond B. Blakney, ed. and trans., *Meister Eckhart* (New York: Harper and Row, 1941), p. 128.

10. See Iain Murray, *The Puritan Hope* (London: Banner of Truth Trust, 1971).

11. Karl Barth, *Protestant Theology in the Nineteenth Century* (Valley Forge: Judson Press, 1973), p. 134.

12. Karl Barth, *The Word of God and the Word of Man,* trans. Douglas Horton (New York: Harper and Row, 1956), p. 276.

13. See Bengt Hägglund, "The Background of Luther's Doctrine of Justification in Late Medieval Theology," *Lutheran World* 8, no. 112 (June 1961): 24–46.

14. Cf. Jürgen Moltmann: "The apostolic succession is, in fact and in truth, the evangelical succession, the continuing and unadulterated proclamation of the gospel of the risen Christ." In *The Church in the Power of the Spirit* (New York: Harper and Row, 1977), p. 359.

15. Hans Küng, *The Church,* trans. Ray and Rosaleen Ockenden (New York: Sheed & Ward, 1967), pp. 354–59.

16. Ibid., p. 219.

17. Dietrich Bonhoeffer, *The Cost of Discipleship,* trans. R.H. Fuller (London: SCM Press Ltd., 1959), p. 151.

18. This same tendency can be observed in the Taizé community, a a

Reformed monastery in France, which seeks to incorporate into its worship life elements from Protestantism, Roman Catholicism, and Eastern Orthodoxy.

19. P.T. Forsyth, *The Justification of God* (London: Independent Press Ltd., 1948), p. 220.

9. A Call to Church Authority
by

JON BRAUN

Jon Braun is a member of the General Council of the New Covenant Apostolic Order and teaches at the Academy of Orthodox Theology in Goleta, California, a school of the Order. He earned the B.D. at North Park Theological Seminary. His first book is It Ain't Gonna Reign No More *(Nashville: Thomas Nelson, 1978).*

We deplore our disobedience to the Lordship of Christ as expressed through authority in his church. This has promoted a spirit of autonomy in persons and groups resulting in isolationism and competitiveness, even anarchy, within the body of Christ. We regret that in the absence of godly authority, there have arisen legalistic, domineering leaders on the one hand and indifference to church discipline on the other.

Therefore we affirm that all Christians are to be in practical submission to one another and to designated leaders in a church under the Lordship of Christ. The church, as the people of God, is called to be the visible presence of Christ in the world. Every

Christian is called to active priesthood in worship and service through exercising spiritual gifts and ministries. In the church we are in vital union both with Christ and with one another. This calls for community with deep involvement and mutual commitment of time, energy and possessions. Further, church discipline, biblically based and under the direction of the Holy Spirit, is essential to the well-being and ministry of God's people. Moreover, we encourage all Christian organizations to conduct their activities with genuine accountability to the whole church.

When Jesus the Son of God walked the earth in His human body, He proclaimed good news, the gospel. In the Gospel of Matthew we are told that He came saying, " 'Repent, for the kingdom of heaven is at hand' " (Matt. 3:2; 4:17). His statement in Mark's Gospel directly connects the kingdom and the gospel: ". . . 'The time is fulfilled, and the kingdom of God is at hand; repent, and believe in the gospel' " (Mark 1:14,15).

Something is clearly implied in those statements that carries the content of the gospel far beyond the point at which many leave it today. Is the gospel the fact that "Jesus died on the cross to save you from your sins"? Yes and no. Yes, that truth is part of the gospel, but no, that is not the whole of the gospel. When we come to the end of the Book of the Acts of the Apostles we find Paul "preaching the *kingdom* of God, and teaching concerning the *Lord* Jesus Christ . . . (Acts 28:31, NASB, italics mine). Sure, Paul preached that Jesus died for our sins. But he was also teaching that Jesus Christ is Lord, is King, and that His kingship could be experienced in part right now. That is what Jesus Himself taught: His kingdom is now and is to come. (A simple definition for *kingdom* would be *the government of God*.) The kingdom to come is experienced in a new heaven and a new earth while the kingdom that is now is primarily experienced in the church.

The Visible Reign of Christ in the World

A Pharisee, Nicodemus, heard Jesus' words "loud and clear": ". . . 'Truly, truly, I say to you, unless one is born again, he cannot see the kingdom of God' " (John 3:3, NASB). Being "born again" was not the *end* in sight. It was the *means* to the end. The end was entering the kingdom of God, which included entering the family of God, the church, the body of Christ.[1] That body considers Jesus Christ to be its Head, its Lord, its King. It is His church, and He rules over it.

There are many who call Him "Lord" but do not acknowledge any visible government over His church. They stop at "being born again" and never practically enter the kingdom. Indeed, from the heavy emphasis on Christian individualism that exists in the twentieth century, one might conclude that there is no practical experience of the kingdom in this life, and that our Lord Jesus Christ has been deposed or is in exile in heaven leaving His people scattered, each one on his own.

But wait! The return of Jesus Christ to the Father was not a trip into exile. You have often heard the expression that Jesus Christ "sitteth at the right hand of the Father, from whence He shall come to judge the quick and the dead." Some conceive that "sitting" to imply a resting, a waiting, till the "fullness of time" has come when "He will reign forever and ever." But in this usage, "sit" is a technical word used as of a king who ascends a throne in order to actively reign over his kingdom. The monarch is seated and begins his reign. Yes, our Lord ascended into heaven from the Mount of Olives to actively reign over His kingdom. " 'He is the one whom God exalted to His right hand as a Prince and a Savior . . .' " (Acts 5:31, NASB). His kingship isn't reserved for the future only. He reigns over His people right now. This implies a government organized among His people. Whoever heard of a great king who reigned or could reign without a government?

Or perhaps each individual Christian is his own private pocket of the kingdom of God, taking all his direction straight from the King with no one else involved at all. It has seemed at times that many Christians have believed that. Do you? Do you envision your experience of the lordship of Christ as limited exclusively to Him and you alone? Then perhaps *you* are the one who is in exile! That is where Christian individualism leads. Oh, you may have good reasons for going it alone. Perhaps you were driven there by some unfortunate circumstances. Or maybe the church to which you belonged was inept and spiritually destitute. So, concluding that this must be the case with all churches, you figured you would be better off on your own, just you and God. Deep inside, however, you knew that the reign of Christ was more than a personal and private matter and that it involves a corporate body. The fact of the matter is there is no way to fully experience the present lordship of Jesus Christ outside of His good government.

Christ's Reign in the Church/Authoritative Leadership

Where, then, is His active reign being expressed today? In the church. And if you don't see His reign expressed in your church, don't conclude that such a reign doesn't exist. For it does. Churches exist where the Lord Jesus Christ is exercising His rule through the authority of godly leaders, leaders who use their authority in the service and care of their people. In such churches individuals are not losing their individuality. Quite to the contrary, they are gaining it and in the process are becoming creative and fulfilled. This is happening through the exercise of godly authority where the people submit to that kind of authority, anticipating it, expecting it, and receiving it. And in doing so they experience the lordship of Jesus Christ.

Today, as in all periods of the history of the church, Jesus Christ is expressing His lordship in churches where there is a proper, godly, serving leadership. In those churches the leaders do not exercise authority as their right, for their own ends, or as an end in itself. Rather, they exercise it as they are directed by the King Himself. Such a leadership looks continually to Him for His direction in the church.

Oh, what peace and joy and blessing when Christ actually and truly reigns in His church! People experience the comfort and joy of salvation and godly living. His purposes are shown in the lives and works of His people. The poor, the widowed, the oppressed, and the orphans receive care.

Every halfway decent civil government that has ever existed on the face of the earth has considered its prime responsibility to be the welfare of its citizenry. Service and administrative officers are appointed at all levels to guard and guide the people. Thus, for example, governmental officials formulate rules for traffic, governmental workers set up stop signs, and police officers make certain that people obey the rules and signs. All of this activity is a normal part of looking after the welfare of the people.

It is certainly no less true that the citizens of the kingdom of God are cared for by their Lord. He, too, appoints representatives. The evidence of His reign through a government was there from the very beginning of the church, with apostles, elders, deacons and others forming a government with authority derived from Christ the King and directed by Him. That made for an actual reign of the Lord in the church.

Authority and Leadership in the New Testament

That there was an authoritative designated leadership in the first-century church is quite apparent from the Scriptures. Paul exhorted the Ephesian elders, " 'Be on guard for yourselves and for all the flock, among which the Holy Spirit has made you overseers . . .' " (Acts 20:28, NASB). To the Corinthians he wrote, "Now I urge you, brethren (you know the household of Stephanas, that they were the first fruits of Achaia, and that they have devoted themselves for ministry to the saints), that you be in subjection to such men and to everyone who helps in the work and labors" (1 Cor. 16:15,16, NASB). And to the church in Thessalonica the charge was given, "But we request of you brethren, that you appreciate those who diligently labor among you, and have charge over you in the Lord . . ." (1 Thess. 5:12, NASB). Young Timothy was reminded by Paul that "the elders who *rule well* be considered worthy of double honor . . ." (1 Tim. 5:17, NASB, italics mine).

Writing to the people of God scattered throughout Pontus,

Galatia, Cappadocia, Asia, and Bythinia, the apostle Peter exhorted the elders to, "shepherd the flock of God among you, not under compulsion, but voluntarily, according to the will of God; . . . nor yet as lording it over those allotted to your charge . . ." (1 Pet. 5:1–3, NASB). He immediately followed this exhortation to the elders with strong words for the young men, "You younger men, likewise, be subject to your elders . . ." (1 Pet. 5:5, NASB).

Then in the Epistle to the Hebrews, the people of the city of God were admonished, "Obey your leaders, and submit to them; for they keep watch over your souls, as those who will give an account . . ." (Heb. 13:17, NASB).

Leadership and Authority in the Generation Following the Apostles

Nor did those who immediately succeeded the apostles fail to see and teach the need for an authoritative and designated leadership in the church. In the twilight years of the first century, an insurrection against the designated leadership occurred in the church at Corinth. Clement, an elder in the church in Rome, writing for that church, challenged those responsible for the revolt with these words:

> Hence you who are the instigators of the revolt must submit to the elders and accept discipline in repentance, bending the knees of your hearts. Learn obedience, laying aside the arrogance and proud willfulness of your tongue.[2]

No more than two or three decades later, Ignatius, bishop of Antioch, the city from which Paul and Barnabas were sent out as apostles just sixty years earlier, wrote the following exhortation in a letter to the Magnesian Christians. His letter had been occasioned by a recent meeting with their bishop, two of their elders, and one of their deacons:

> Since, then, in the persons already mentioned I have beheld the whole congregation in faith and have loved it, I exhort you: be eager to do everything in harmony, with the bishop presiding in the place of God and the presbytery in the place of the council of

the apostles and the deacons, most sweet to me, entrusted with the service of Jesus Christ—who before the ages was with the Father and was made manifest at the end.[3]

Leadership and Authority into Reformation Times

Almost no one would question that the ancient church of the Fathers recognized a strong, authoritative, designated leadership. So did the high medieval church. But this was also true in Reformation times. In his *Apology of the Augsburg Confession,* the Reformer-theologian Philip Melanchthon followed suit with the New Testament church and the church of the times of the Fathers:

According to the Gospel, therefore, only those are the true people who accept the promise of the Spirit. Besides the church is the kingdom of Christ, the opposite of the kingdom of the devil.[4]

The Lutheran's Augsburg Confession itself is quite to the point with respect to authoritative leadership in the church.[5] The Reformed confessions also strongly confess such a leadership.[6]

Leadership and Authority in Modern Times

Oddly, it is only in modern times that there has been widespread resistance to leadership with authority in the church. Authoritative leadership has come on hard times. The spirit of the age calls for weak leadership—or no leadership at all. The consequences of such a collapse of effective authority in the church are manifold. Four stand out with particular significance.

1. *A weak leadership produces autonomous people.* When authority, properly constituted and exercised in a godly manner, is weak or missing, the door is swung open for the spirit of autonomy to walk in. People who are not properly led and guided naturally take over the direction of their own lives.

We've seen this "personal take-over" exemplified many times in the history of civil governments. When there is a breakdown in national authority and contradictory orders are issued by local civil servants, confidence in the stability of the government is shaken. Revolution or anarchy may result. Similarly, when church leaders are divided, the people lack confidence. The members of that body head in all different directions. Splintering and dissipation of the energy of the church result because this autonomy infects both individuals and groups. Almost of necessity there develops the subtle attitude that "we can make it on our own because whom can we trust to lead us according to the Lord's will?" Under such circumstances believers may still experience some degree of God's blessing in a personal way, but there will be little actual experience of His sovereign kingship.

This spirit of autonomy has many other sad consequences for the church. Isolationism and competitiveness develop within the body of Christ. I am reminded of what happens in a nation whose civil government is destroyed by war or insurrection. People trust nobody and barricade their homes. Local leaders develop competing governments. Eventually, people decide that no government is better than poor government. Chaos and anarchy result.

So it can become among the people of the great kingdom. Each individual or group becomes, in effect, its own little kingdom of God. Each sees itself in competition with the other groups surrounding it. Anarchy prevails as each Christian comes to believe that he has to have his own answers and behave according to the dictates of his own conscience. Such is the case far too often in modern evangelicalism.

Tragically, then, the spirit of autonomy freezes people into their own little world, takes away the very freedom autonomy promises, and prevents them from experiencing the active reign and rule of Christ. Make no mistake about it: Jesus Christ the Lord *is* reigning in His church, but like it or not, those who are seduced by the spirit of autonomy *are not* living under that reign.

2. *A divided leadership produces a divided church.* The spirit of autonomy has pervaded even the leadership of the church. As

a result the leadership itself is divided. The plain fact is that most of the problems and divisions that exist in the twentieth-century church are caused by weak and divided leadership. The sheep are divided because the shepherds stand apart.

It is at the most crucial level, the local level, that divisions of Christendom are not only most apparent but also most destructive. Here we have the paradox of, let us say, fifteen churches in a five square mile area, often with their buildings sitting side by side. Each is governed separately from the others, often by an outside national headquarters. Think what it would mean in civil government to have competing governmental structures in the same territory!

Anciently, the church was unified locally under the leadership of its bishops.[7] Today, at least in America, there is no territorial unity in the church. Indeed the ancient concept of the reign of Christ through leaders who see and hear from Him through the Holy Spirit has altogether disappeared from large segments of the church.

3. *Government by law.* This is another tragic consequence of the collapse of an authoritative, designated leadership in the church. A naive approach to authority in the church has arisen in the place of an authoritative leadership: moderately authoritative legalism. Following the lead of secular government, church leaders have turned to a government by rules and regulations. Many have every intent to govern according to directives from the Lord, but they end up with a legalistic and domineering system. They counsel, they interpret, they direct on the basis of principles and policies rather than on the basis of seeing and hearing from the reigning Lord through His Spirit. Thus, many churches and groups that belong to Christ the King are governed by following systems of laws rather than by obeying His voice.

Unfortunately, leaders who "go by the book," turning to some rather ill-defined system of laws rather than to the Lawgiver, tend to be domineering and arbitrary. They are domineering because they blanket their people with laws and weigh them down with rules that have nothing to do with the reign of Christ. They are arbitrary in that they usually retreat to the "safe" position of doing nothing when confronted by a situation not covered by the rules. The Lord once said of the Pharisees, " 'And they tie up heavy loads, and lay them on men's shoulders; but they themselves are unwilling to move them with so much as a finger' " (Matt. 23:4, NASB).

4. *The disappearance of effective church discipline.* The absence of proper godly authority (coupled with our horrendous divisions) has given rise to a widespread indifference to church discipline.[8] Some of us are naturally rebellious, and rebellious types are always looking for some excuse to turn away. Anarchists will use any lever possible to overthrow authority, good or bad. This is nothing new: The church has always been faced by such people, but it seems that our contemporary church is especially plagued by them. Whether authority is good or evil is irrelevant to such people. Wolves will kick at and scoff any kind of authority.

When a church attempts to discipline a rebel, he either raises an internal rebellion or storms off saying something such as, "I'll just find another church to fellowship with!" Unfortunately, that is all too possible in our modern scene. Again, the reign of Christ is mocked.

But for sincere and good people, a proper, orderly, godly discipline is a blessing. They respond to it in a positive manner, recognizing that the Lord disciplines everyone He receives. Faithful discipline administered by godly authority is a vital aspect of the active reign of the Lord Jesus Christ in His church. Weak and divided authority promotes indifference to church discipline, and good people will either leave and look for godly leaders, or decide there is no such thing.

Proper Characteristics of an Authoritative Leadership

What is involved in godly authority? If the church is the place where the Lord Jesus Christ reigns through godly leadership, what then should characterize that authority?

Leadership Does Not Establish Itself

Leadership in the church is never to be self-appointed. No one is to promote himself to the top. Unfortunately, however, this happens too often in today's church, and such an inept practice will produce either impotent leadership on the one hand or tyrannical leadership on the other. The plight of numerous churches and Christian organizations testifies to this fact.

A leader must be established by an authority outside of himself. The contention, "God alone established me," will not do. I do not intend to cavil here over differences between conflicting theories of church government. Personally, I prefer a combination of Episcopal, Presbyterian, and Congregational. That comes out to the appointing or recognizing of leadership by the existing leadership, but with the hearty recommendation and "amen" of the people. Be that as it may, leadership must be established by authority whether that authority be in an office or embodied in the congregation. *It takes authority to establish authority.*

One critical side effect of authority establishing authority is the occasional need to remove a leader in the church. Leadership in the church must not have a guaranteed tenure. Any leader who for one reason or another can't, won't, or isn't fit to fulfil his role of leadership must be removed from his office. Too often the church of God has operated on one cylinder because of leadership that will not function properly and will not step aside. Such leadership must be removed.

Leadership is dismissed in a manner similar to the way it is established. This should involve at least two factors. First, the authority that established the leader in question must do the dismissing. It takes authority to dismiss authority. Yet, second, there must be a provision for the people who are to be served to give input that may affect any decision regarding the dismissal of a leader. (Of course it is virtually impossible to remove unacceptable leaders in a structure where there is no accountability, or where accountability is extremely weak or ill-defined.)

Leadership Itself Must Be Under Authority.

Remember the centurion Jesus encountered? "For I too am a man under authority." Being under authority, he could exercise authority and also recognize someone else in the same position.

Perhaps you have heard some Christian leader say something to the effect, "Everyone in this group should submit to me." In such a group people who desire to live under the reign of Christ need to know the answer to a question: "To whom does this leader submit?" If his answer is, "I submit to God only," beware! He who tells others what to do needs to demonstrate that he, too, can follow orders. And not only that he did once-upon-a-time, but that he still does. He who expects obedience must know by experience what obedience is like. He needs to be in a practical and working submission either to peers or to someone over him in leadership. In the ancient church this was made actual by bishops submitting to neighboring bishops so that no one was left unprotected. The modern church has the strong tendency to leave its top leadership unaccountable.

Leaders in the Lord's church must be submissive. This is for their protection and service as well as for the service and protection of the people under their care. Well-intentioned people can take advantage of an unprotected leader. A very few can dominate all his time and energies. Meanwhile, the rest of the flock remain unshepherded for all practical purposes. Further, if such a leader sincerely desires to do the best for his people, the devil will constantly attack him concerning the adequacy of his leadership. How can he be so sure that he is doing the right thing? Guilt and uncertainty about his decisions will eat away at his heart.

On the other hand, if he is truly answerable, he has someone with whom to consult, someone with whom he can turn to the

Lord to find His will in every situation. Only then can those haunting accusations be adequately handled.

Leadership has been called a lonely role, but it should not be that way. Leaders who carry on their ministry under proper godly authority in the church have the privilege of experiencing the workings of that authority themselves. It has a source, the Lord Himself; it has order as He Himself directs; and it has a goal, the welfare of the people of the kingdom.

The Speaking Holy Spirit

Leadership must get its content and direction from the Lord Himself. This is accomplished through the person of the Holy Spirit.

God never intended for us to have to figure out on our own how to govern the church. First, godly authority is the authority of Christ working in the church. That means a living connection with Him, a connection through which the leadership (operating in conjunction with all of the people) actively see and hear from Him. Contrary to much of our present-day experience, the Holy Spirit is alive and speaking today!

In a vast secular government, civil leaders must rely on law, because they are unable to consult constantly with their king, their president, or their prime minister. This does not need to be so in the government of Jesus Christ. For Christ has said, "But when He, the Spirit of truth, comes, He will guide you into all the truth; for He will not speak on His own initiative, but whatever He hears, He will speak; and He will disclose to you what is to come. He shall glorify Me; for He shall take of Mine, and shall disclose it to you. All things that the Father has are Mine; therefore I said, that He takes of Mine, and will disclose it to you" (John 16:13–15, NASB). Properly oriented leaders in the church can see and hear from the Lord. They can know Him personally and walk with Him in an ever-deepening relationship. Then, when situations arise in the lives of individual members which require decisions, such leaders are able to receive direction from the Lord.

But a church is more than its leadership. The Lord's desire is that all the members see and hear from Him. A church with input only from the top is a church without proper authority. What the Lord says to others is neglected. In a church under proper authority, input from the Holy Spirit can be received through *any* member. When individual members believe that God has revealed something to them they can take it to their leaders for judgment. In such a context leaders need not be threatened by a word coming from the flock. They can take it, consider it prayerfully, and judge whether or not it is truly from the Lord. We must understand that the presence of the Holy Spirit in the church means that sometimes the entire church can be led in a direction that eventually is brought to judgment by a member who might, in worldly eyes, seem the lowliest. No, leaders in the church do not need to assume that they will be the only ones who hear from the Lord. Such an attitude would be fatal to the reign of Christ. All must be heard. In effect every member participates in the government of the church.

Service and Care

Godly, authoritative, designated leadership must administer service and care to the people it governs.

Under prevailing cultural attitudes toward leadership, many see authority as an opportunity to dominate. That's the way it has often been in this world. But the Lord at the beginning of His church said it had to be different among us: "Jesus called them to Himself, and said, 'You know that the rulers of the Gentiles lord it over them, and their great men exercise authority over them. It is not so among you, but whoever wishes to become great among you shall be your servant, and whoever wishes to be first among you shall be your slave; just as the Son of Man did not come to be served, but to serve, and to give His life a ransom for many'" (Matt. 20:25–28, NASB).

It is one thing to tell people in the church what to do. It is quite another both to tell them what to do and to serve and care for them in the process. For example, a father who tells his children to do good to others but doesn't also serve and care for his children has a family heading for trouble. An ungodly authority does not provide service and care. Unfortunately, many church leaders today are living under the deception that care means only preaching the Word to the people. But listen, please: Care involves far more than preaching the Word. It does involve that, but it includes much more.

Being a church involves being a family. Caring for a church is similar to caring for a family as a father does. If all a father did was preach to his family (and he certainly needs to do that), he would be a failure. A good father also provides for the well-being of his family, physically, mentally, emotionally, and spiritually. He sees to it that his children are fully developed in all aspects of their lives. His children become creative, productive, and fulfilled. They also see in their father an example of service and care that they can follow in their own lives.

It's the same in the church. A proper, godly authority preaches to, provides for, and develops its people as fully as possible. What follows in that church is an example of the reign of Christ. The people pick up that spirit of service and care from their leaders, and great are the benefits to all concerned.

Discipline

Godly leadership must provide discipline in the church. The people of God under the reign of Christ must be a disciplined body. Individuals must be guided in the proper direction in all areas of their lives. The church as a whole must function as a co-ordinated organism, doing the will of the Lord. A godly leadership is the instrument by which the Lord provides that discipline.

Discipline requires training. No one automatically lives a disciplined life and no church automatically behaves in a disciplined fashion. The people of God are shown by their leaders how to develop healthy, productive, and fulfilled lives. Training and instruction in godly living must be a regular function of church leadership.

Discipline also involves correction. Even Christian people fall into sin and improper habits of life. They have to change. Correction may be needed in almost any area of life: morals, use of money, use of time, social relationships, intellectual pursuits, vocation, family relationships, relationship with God. Most of us would say that a father who does not properly discipline his children is a bad father. Similarly, church leaders who do not properly discipline their flocks are poor leaders.

Godly Behavior

The leadership itself must be characterized by virtue.

The apostle Peter gave some instruction concerning Christian virtues: "Now for this very reason also, applying all diligence, in your faith supply moral excellence, and in your moral excellence, knowledge; and in your knowledge, self-control, and in your self-control, perseverance, and in your perseverance, godliness; and in your godliness, brotherly kindness, and in your brotherly kindness, Christian love. For if these qualities are yours and are increasing, they render you neither useless nor unfruitful in the true knowledge of our Lord Jesus Christ" (2 Pet. 1:5–8, NASB). If these seven qualities are to be exhibited by Christians, should they not first be seen in the lives of their leaders?

Moral excellence or virtue is an absolute essential. A Christian leader who lives an immoral life is more than a disgrace, he is a shameful disaster to the church. In his marital relationship, his business relationships, in all his dealings, he of all people should be unquestionably clean. He is an example to the flock and to the world. All too many have seen Christian leaders involved in adultery, caught up in shady business deals, and drowned in their own deceptions. That sort of thing is destructive to the reign of Christ.

Knowledge of God, of the Scriptures, and an orthodox interpretation of those Scriptures, is indispensable to the Christian leader. Guardianship of apostolic doctrine lies in the hands of the leadership of the church. Of course we do not all have the same mental capacity and we must not place the highest value on those with the most knowledge, but here is an area in which laziness and indifference is utterly intolerable. Christian leaders must know the truth in order to teach the truth and combat error.

It seems *self-control* is out of style in our get-it-while-the-getting-is-good society. Nevertheless, no Christian leader should be without it. Self-control involves control of the passions. For example, let's take the passion of eating. A godly leader needs to be in control of the amount of food he takes in. Let's face it, overweight leaders betray the fact that they have lost control of the passion of hunger. Confidence in authoritative leadership is difficult to maintain when the passions of leaders themselves appear to be out from under the lordship of Christ.

Perseverance is another often-neglected virtue among Christian leaders today. Too many leaders "opt out" when the going gets tough. Oh, they usually don't leave the ministry, but when difficulties arise they conveniently decide that the problems mean God is calling them to a different pastorate. Godly leadership calls for sticking it out and caring for people in the face of opposition and adversity.

Every Christian leader should be an example of *godliness.* This implies a willingness to receive from the Lord and practise those God-like characteristics of purity of life and thought that are available only from Him. A Christian leader must genuinely love his Lord and his flock enough to want to be like the Lord.

Of course *brotherly kindness* is necessary to the leader who is going to serve and care for people. Godly leaders cherish their people and treat them with tenderness. To cherish is to value highly. Tenderness means to handle gently. The shepherding illustration is valuable here. Sheep need to be highly valued and handled gently if they are to prosper. They thrive in such an atmosphere. It's the same with the Lord's people in His church. It's wrong to treat them roughly and crush them in the pretext of "doing it for their own good." Christ nourishes and cherishes His church through those whom He has appointed as shepherds in His church.

Finally, there is *love*. That virtue, received from the Lord, is essential in the Christian leader. One aspect of it is the cherishing and tenderness we've just noted. But there is more to love. Love is also firm. People are not served with love if there is not firmness in carrying out the work of the Lord. Further, they are not going to respect "wishy-washy" leaders. The love of such leaders is suspect. Some leaders are afraid to be firm because they're afraid they might be wrong. Well, they might be. Godly leaders are not infallible. They sometimes make mistakes, but when they do, they can apologize and make amends. Nevertheless, the direction they provide will be safe and sound overall, and no one will suffer unduly from the minor errors they make. When they are convinced that they have the will of the Lord in a given situation, they need to stand firmly. Otherwise the leadership will lose credibility.

The Church and Its Authority

Up to this point we have primarily emphasized the role of the leadership with respect to authority in the church. Let's turn the coin over and look at the role of the church in relation to authority.

The church, as the apostle Peter said, is an active priesthood: "But you are a chosen race, a royal priesthood, a holy nation, a people for God's own possession, that you may proclaim the excellencies of Him who has called you out of darkness into His marvelous light . . ." (1 Pet. 2:9, NASB). The priesthood is not one segment of the church opposed to another segment. The clergy do not, as some seem to assume, constitute all the priesthood by themselves. We must grasp the fact that the entire church is the priesthood.

This priesthood exercises spiritual gifts and ministries both in worship and in service. It has been said that the wealth of any nation is summed up in its people and its natural resources. Well, the wealth of any church is summed up in its people and its natural and supernatural resources, that is, the people with their talents, spiritual gifts, and ministries.

If, as we sometimes see, only the leadership is considered to be the priesthood, then only the leadership will exercise gifts and ministries. The consequences are grave and far-reaching. First, though not most important, the leadership is stifled and smothered by having to do the vast majority of the work. But more importantly, few gifts are developed, the people are not spiritually developed and fulfilled, and their gifts go down the drain. Thus the people of the church suffer, and the Lord's will is not done by the church in the world.

Whose fault is it? Well, we could spread the blame out pretty far, but blame is not our purpose. We do know it is the responsibility of the leadership of the church to develop the people and utilize their resources in doing the work that the Lord gives to His church.

Authority Involves Submission

But even the most godly, perceptive, diligent leadership depends upon the willingness of the people to do what the Lord tells them. There is a word that has been much thrown about, much abused, and little understood: *submission*. Many are saying today, "You must be in submission in the church," or, "You can't be in the Lord's will unless you're in submission somewhere." Most of us wonder what on earth they mean. Besides, the word *submission* gives us all kinds of frightening vibrations of weakness, oppression, and slavery.

Dictionary definitions of submission center on the concept of yielding in surrender or obedience. Now, in the first place, our contemporary, national cultural ideology is against the whole idea of yielding or surrendering to anything or anybody. Second, our heritage has also ingrained in us a hatred of oppression. We don't want to be run over by anybody. Thus the negative connotation of the word *submission*.

The fact is, however, that despite our ideology, we all do submit—every day. We submit to the laws and leadership of our nation, our state, our city. We yield, comply, and obey. At work we do the same. Our boss or his representative says, "This is what you will do and these are the boundaries within which you will do it." So we do. We know that if people do not obey the government of the nation, chaos will result. We know that if we do not obey our employer, we will be fired. So we submit.

But somehow when it comes to submission in the church, our hackles rise. There are a number of reasons why we find submission to be viewed in a different manner in the church. Some of us have been taught that Christianity is an individual religion in which all that matters is your "relationship with God." Some Christian leaders have made submission abhorrent by their abuse of authority. There is also an awe at the tremendous power that could exist in the church with a dedicated congregation thoroughly submitted to a strong leadership.

None of these reasons, however, even begins to compete with the reasons *for* submitting ourselves in the church wholeheartedly. The Lord once said to Moses regarding Israel, ". . . I have seen this people, and behold, they are an obstinate [or stiff necked] people" (Exod. 39:9, NASB). He said it because they had failed to yield to and obey His designated leader, Moses. *We cannot get around the fact that submission to the Lord involves submission to His designated leadership in the church.*

Does that mean, however, that the individual member of the church is expected to wait for orders in his own life from church authority and when he receives them to abjectly obey? No. That defeats the whole idea of the church as the body of Christ, a corporate priesthood. Submission in the church means a wholehearted commitment to enter in, follow the designated leadership, and thereby develop and utilize one's natural and spiritual gifts. It means taking the role that is agreed upon as ours and acting upon the decisions made in the church generally, and with respect to our lives in particular.

Those who in this way genuinely submit to their God-ordained leaders have the fullest and richest life possible ahead of them. As a priesthood knit together in the love of Christ, a church made up of such people will see their gifts and ministries developed to the fullest potential. Such a priesthood will worship the Lord in honor and thanksgiving. It will become rich in service expressed in good works toward both its own members and people outside the church.

The entire church constitutes the priesthood. But it is not a leaderless priesthood. It is an authoritatively led priesthood. Wise leadership will devote itself to the task of bringing to maturity the gifts and ministries of all who are in submission to Christ's active reign in the church.

Community and Authoritative Leadership

Yet one more need for designated authority in the church is the church's need to fulfill her role as a community. The New Testament presents us with a church that was a community having deep involvement and mutual commitment of time, energy, and possessions on the part of all its members. The lives of its people were utterly intertwined in that community. The community had its own courts, it cared for its own sick, its own orphans, and its own poor. It worshiped together, it often ate together. It even had standards as to how its people should or should not dress. No part of the lives of its people was exempt from the all-encompassing government of God as expressed in the community of the church.

Unfortunately, in our modern culture the church is often seen as little more than a vehicle to minister to the religious life of its people. The result is that the reign of Christ, at least in the church, also extends no further. There is need for little or no authority in a church with such a restricted sphere of ministry.

Such a limited concept of the church is not the church with which we are confronted in the Scriptures. Neither is it the church that can adequately minister amidst the complexities of the twentieth century. As the church in antiquity appropriately met the needs of its people, so also must the church of modernity. In addition to its so-called "spiritual ministry," the church must be concerned with its unemployed, its widows and widowers, and its lonesome children. It must take up the slack when a family doesn't have enough money for its needs. It must see to the care of its sick and its elderly, and be present and ready to help when disaster and misfortune strike. No need of life of its people may be ignored.

This kind of community cannot exist without the presence of godly authority and submission to that authority. In fact such commitment would not be safe. Why? Because apart from the good government of God, some people would rise up to take unfair advantage of others. Mutual love and trust cannot survive apart from such government. Personality conflicts would be unresolved. Impasses would be reached in some relationships. People would become frozen in irreconcilable differences. But godly, diligent authority and submission to that authority provide a place and an atmosphere in which grievances can be aired and where the people can resolve their differences under the gracious reign of Christ.

Leadership and order are required to adequately serve needs. Leadership is needed to correctly apportion resources. Leadership is necessary to determine who should do what and how. Without leadership, care is haphazard and unjust. A church must have designated leadership with authority to survive as a caring community, a productive outpost of the kingdom of God.[9]

Conclusion

We have spoken of the church as the visible presence of Christ in the world, of godly church authority, and of a church's relationship to its authority. We have taken note of the fact that the gospel we preach is the gospel of the kingdom of God, and therefore, that the reign of Christ the Lord in the church must be practical and visible.

Therefore, we affirm that all Christians are to be in practical submission to one another and to designated leaders in a church under the lordship of Christ. Such churches do exist in the world—and may their tribe increase!

We call upon all Christian leaders to be examples of the kind of leadership that exemplifies the visible reign of Christ in the church.

We challenge all of God's people to submit themselves to godly authority in churches under the lordship of Christ. "Obey your leaders, and submit to them; for they keep watch over your souls, as those who will give an account. Let them do this with joy and not with grief, for this would be unprofitable for you" (Heb. 13:17, NASB).

Notes

1. Much has been written concerning the debate over the degree of identity the church has with the kingdom of God. I do not assume a complete identity of the church and the kingdom of God in its totality. However, I do assume that the church is the locus of the Christian's primary experience in this age of the kingdom of God.

2. Jack Sparks, ed., 1 Clement 57, *The Apostolic Fathers,* Nashville: Thomas Nelson, 1978).

3. *Magnesians 6:1,* ibid., vol. IV.

4. *Apology of the Augsburg Confession,* in *The Book of Concord,* ed. Theodore G. Tappert (Philadelphia: Fortress Press, 1959), p. 170.

5. "It is proper for the Christian assembly to keep such ordinances for the sake of love and peace, to be obedient to the bishops and parish ministers in such matters, and to observe the regulations in such a way that one does not give offence to another and so that there may be no disorder or unbecoming conduct in the church." Augsburg Confession, Article XXVIII, from John H. Leith, ed., *Creeds of the Churches,* rev. ed. (Richmond: John Knox Press, 1973), p. 103.

6. The section on "Ministers of the Word" in the Geneva Confession of 1536 is an example. "We recognize no other pastors in the Church than faithful pastors of the Word of God, feeding the sheep of Christ on the one hand with instruction, admonition, consolation, exhortation, deprecation; and on the other resisting all false doctrines and deceptions of the devil, without mixing with the pure doctrine of the Scriptures their dreams or their foolish imaginings." From Arthur C. Cochrane, ed., "The Geneva Confession of 1536," *Reformed Con-*

fessions of the 16th Century (Philadelphia: Westminster Press, 1966), p. 125.

7. Helpful historical discussion of the bishop in the ancient church is found in H.E. Kirk, ed., *The Apostolic Ministry* (London: Hodder and Stoughton, 1946), particularly the essay by Gregory Dix, "The Ministry in the Early Church." Also helpful is Edwin Hatch's 1880 Bampton Lectures, *The Organization of the Early Christian Churches,* and the counterpart of Hatch, R.C. Moberly, *Ministerial Priesthood,* first published 1897, reprinted with a new introduction by A.T. Hanson (London: S.P.C.K., 1969).

8. For an interesting discussion of church discipline see John T. McNeill, *A History of the Cure of Souls* (New York: Harper and Row, 1965).

9. Eric G. Jay, *The Church: Its Changing Image Through Twenty Centuries* (London: S.P.C.K., 1977). In his discussion of the church of the apostolic Fathers, Jay comments: "The authors we have studied in this chapter make it clear that the early church quickly came to realize that its well-being rested not only with the quality of its ministers, but also with their recognition, by the church as a whole, as being properly vested with authority. There cannot long be a healthy life in any community if there are no leaders and servants who are recognized as such by the community" (p. 49).

10. A Call to Church Unity
by
F. Burton Nelson

*F. Burton Nelson is Professor of Theology and
Ethics at North Park Theological Seminary in
Chicago, Illinois. He completed his seminary
work at Yale Divinity School and earned the
Ph.D. from Northwestern University.*

*We deplore the scandalous isolation and separation of Christians from
one another. We believe such division is contrary to Christ's explicit
desire for unity among his people and impedes the witness of the church
in the world. Evangelicalism is too frequently characterized by an
ahistorical, sectarian mentality. We fail to appropriate the catholicity
of historic Christianity, as well as the breadth of the biblical revelation.*

*Therefore we call evangelicals to return to the ecumenical
concern of the Reformers and the later movements of evangelical
renewal. We must humbly and critically scrutinize our respective
traditions, renounce sacred shibboleths, and recognize that God
works within diverse historical streams. We must resist efforts*

promoting church union-at-any-cost, but we must also avoid mere spiritualized concepts of church unity. We are convinced that unity in Christ requires visible and concrete expressions. In this belief, we welcome the development of encounter and cooperation within Christ's church. While we seek to avoid doctrinal indifferentism and a false irenicism, we encourage evangelicals to cultivate increased discussion and cooperation, both within and without their respective traditions, earnestly seeking common areas of agreement and understanding.

The time has come in the chronology of evangelicalism's maturation to consider faithfully and responsibly the call to church unity. The twenty-first century is only two decades away. By the time the new milennium dawns, evangelical Christians should have come a long way toward meeting the several goals enunciated in this reflective essay. Neglect or failure to do so would undoubtedly constitute a serious deafness to what the Lord of the church seems to be saying to the churches in our time.

The twentieth century has been in a significant measure *the* ecumenical century in the evolution of the Christian church. The shattering and the fracturing of the sixteenth century, as well as the proliferation of the intervening centuries, has been met with the reconciling and peacemaking of the twentieth. Evangelical Christians dare not walk by on the other side as if this sifting, shifting, and regrouping is of little or no concern. It is an hour to reflect on the separation of Christians from one another and to deplore scandalous isolation and division.

The Lord of the Church Desires Unity

One of the hallmarks of evangelical Christianity through the years has been the declared intention to be the people of the Book. Evangelicals historically and presently have unreservedly stated their wish to listen to the living Word in the Scripture. The call, therefore, comes today to all evangelicals to search the Scriptures intensively as they seek to articulate the nature of the church and to understand what the church is, including the numerous passages on unity. New Testament language about the church is forthright and positive. Its message about the unity of Christians is definitive: The Lord Jesus Christ, the Ruler of the church, desires the unity of His people.

That unity stood high on the agenda of Jesus' intentions and aspirations for His followers is persuasively evident in the high priestly prayer that He offered just before His death:

> . . . keep them in thy name, which thou hast given me, that they may be one, even as we are one.
>
> —John 17:11
>
> I do not pray for these only, but also for those who believe in me through their word, that they may all be one.
>
> —John 17:20,21

Jesus' prayer is that those who name His name will be marked by oneness. The prayer for unity has an integrity in and of itself; such a unity among His followers is a distinctive way of glorifying God. There is another dimension to it, however. Unity is an instrument to be used in the worldwide mission of the church. Jesus prayed:

> that they may all be one; even as thou, Father, art in me, and I in thee, that they also may be in us, so that the world may believe that thou hast sent me.
>
> —John 17:21
>
> . . . that they may become perfectly one, so that the world may know that thou hast sent me and hast loved them even as thou hast loved me.
>
> —John 17:23

The unity of the people of God is organically related to the proclamation of the Good News. In an important sense, the credibility of the proclamation is dependent upon the impression that is conveyed to people outside the church of how Christians relate to one another. No one can calculate the number of persons who have turned away from the church in disdain and disgust because of the bitterness and the divisiveness among the followers of Christ.

It is not surprising that the first great stimulus toward unity in the twentieth century emerged from the world mission enterprise. Edinburgh (1910), the initial ecumenical conference in this century, resulted from the pleas by missionaries that the scandal of division and disunity among Christians be seriously and soberly examined. They had faced firsthand the importance of Jesus' manifesto: Unity and mission, unity and evangelism, are imperative partners in the spread of the gospel.

The pressing word from the Lausanne Covenant constitutes a reminder of this affirmation to all evangelical Christians today:

> Evangelism also summons us to unity, because our oneness strengthens our witness, just as our disunity undermines our gospel of reconciliation.[1]

New Testament language about unity is forcefully conveyed in the letters of Paul. The Ephesian letter offers the classic description of this unity (esp. 4:4–6). Like a symphonic theme, this note of oneness is sounded: one body, one Spirit, one hope, one Lord, one faith, one baptism, one God and Father of us all. The language is declarative, as it is also in many other passages: Our unity in Christ is *given*. It is pure gift. It is of the very essence of the church to be one. It is inherent in the call to be Christian.

The Corinthian letters, moreover, are significant in Paul's case for unity among Christians. He upbraids those who cause quarreling and dissension (1 Cor. 1:10–17) and urges that ". . . you be united in the same mind and the same judgment" (1 Cor. 1:10). He uses the language of the body, the one and the many, to capture the unity and the multiplicity of the members (1 Cor. 12:12–14,27).

In our modern individualistic bias, we could easily by-pass the primary thrust of Paul's perspective. As Eduard Schweizer has put it:

The Corinthians are fundamentally and primarily the Body of Christ, and only in a secondary way individual members. (v. 27) The main reality is the oneness of Christ's body. The individuality of the members is only a secondary characteristic of the one body. . . . We shall never understand Paul's concept of the church if we begin our theological thinking with the individual Christian and consider the church as something like a social gathering or an association of individuals sharing some common interests.[2]

This is then one of the bulwark facets of New Testament teaching about church unity that invites reflection: As we hear and heed the call of Christ, we enter into a relationship with Christ; we are joined to Christ. But there is more. We are joined to one another also in Christ. We are given to each other in Christ whether we acknowledge it or identify with it or not. Our unity is God's free gift, and we belong to one another for eternity. This must have been the vision that Dietrich Bonhoeffer sought to convey in the early stages of the church struggle in Germany as he reflected on "community":

Christianity means community through Jesus Christ and in Jesus Christ. No Christian community is more or less than this. Whether it be a brief, single encounter or the daily fellowship of years, Christian community is only this. We belong to one another only through and in Jesus Christ.[3]

Much of the New Testament language about the church may tell us more about unity if we can hear the beat of a drummer other than that of individualism. All of these images call for pondering and reflecting in the light of the unity of God's own people:

> One body and many members (Rom. 12:4,5)
> One building of many stones (1 Pet. 2:5)
> One vine and many branches (John 15:1–10)
> One people of God (1 Pet. 2:9,10)
> One fellowship of faith (1 John 1)
> One household of God (1 Pet. 4:17)

In Paul Minear's monumental study, *Images of the Church in the New Testament,* [4] most of the analogies appear to have the theme of unity as a significant dimension of the meaning. Here, too, the theme is repeated: Unity is first and foremost a "given." It is not simply a goal to be attained and achieved; it is a gift to be received and then cultivated.

The Christians in each geographical location represent the one church of Christ in the world. Each congregation or assembly is a kind of microcosm of the whole *ecclesia.* Paul did not seem to get caught in the local/universal dichotomy. His salutations are revealing commentaries on this theme: "the church of God which is at Corinth"; "to the church of the Thessalonians"; "the church in your house."

As evangelical Christians discuss the character of the New Testament language about unity, as they confront anew the Lord's desire for unity, and as they wrestle with implications for the life and work of the church today, incessant questions call for responses:

> What *is* this unity about which the New Testament speaks? Is it only or primarily a *spiritual* unity that has no necessary consequence in visible experience?
>
> If unity is genuinely a gift, what shall we make of the divisions and separations of the churches today? Are they "shameful disgrace" or "healthy diversity"? Are they scandalous?
>
> Where is the body of Christ today? Where do we truly find the boundaries of this body?

Church Unity and Evangelical Roots

Evangelical Christians are not only marked by a declared intention to be the people of the Book. Our own history has been substantially rooted in ecumenical concern. As we consider the contemporary call to church unity, therefore, it is not only the Scriptures that must be searched; evangelical traditions also must be searched and sifted.

The Reformation

The Reformation of the sixteenth century has sometimes been interpreted as a shattering of the church's unity. The Reformers themselves are perceived as sectarians who recklessly tore the fabric of the church into a thousand fragments. The Reformation is thereby presented as the ultimate in individualism, each person possessing "the right of private judgment." Such a twisted interpretation is a gross misconception of the truth. On the contrary, the Reformers were vitally and deeply concerned about the unity of the body, and they taught this unity as an integral part of the church's essential nature.

A clarion voice for this perspective is that of John T. McNeill, the Protestant church historian. In his convincing book, *Unitive Protestantism: The Ecumenical Spirit and Its Persistent Expression,* Dr. McNeill contends that "the ideal of Christian unity was a pronounced original characteristic of Protestantism."[5]

> Protestantism, while not unaffected by the nationalistic and individualistic movements that preceded and accompanied it, possessed an inward unitive principle by virtue of which it resisted with a measure of success, the forces of disintegration. The assertion of this principle by the Reformers is indicated with reference to their teaching on the communion of believers, their claim of catholicity against the sectarianism of Rome, and their conciliar ideal of church government.[6]

Martin Luther, consequently, can be pictured in this stream of interpretation as a champion of the church's essential unity, despite an occasional outburst or invective which was this inimitable churchman's stock in trade.

> Luther and his fellow Reformers always insisted that they were not establishing a new church. Whenever the suspicion arose that they were doing this, they reacted with strong feelings. In 1522 Luther wrote: "In the first place, I ask that men make no reference to my name, let them call themselves Christians, not Lutherans. What is Luther? After all the teaching is not mine. Neither was I crucified for anyone. St. Paul in I Corinthians 3

would not allow the Christians to call themselves Pauline or Petrine, but Christian. How then should I—poor stinking maggot-fodder that I am—come to have men call the children of Christ by my wretched name? Not so, my dear friends; let us abolish all party names and call ourselves Christians, after him whose teaching we hold . . . I neither am nor want to be anyone's master." This sentiment can be found repeatedly in Luther's writings. The first Lutheran was not a sectarian but an ecumenist![7]

Neither Luther, nor any of the magisterial Reformers, intended to carve the body of Christ into segments. At the very outset of Luther's reform was the conference in the interests of unity at Marburg in 1529. It is true that consensus was not reached on all points, but it is nonetheless remarkable that of the fifteen articles framed by Luther, fourteen did receive agreement.

Luther continuously throughout his career as pastor, teacher, and churchman, sought to uphold the unity of all believers. His 1520 exposition of the Apostles' Creed states:

> I believe that there is on earth, as wide as the world, no more than one holy, universal Christian Church, which is nothing else than the community or congregation of the saints, i.e. of all the devout, believing men on earth. This church is gathered, kept, and ruled by the Holy Spirit, and daily increased by the sacraments and the Word of God.[8]

That this note was continued in the Lutheran documents is evident from the Augsburg Confession of 1530. Article VII confesses:

> It is enough for the true unity of the Christian Church that the Gospel be preached in accordance with pure doctrine and the sacraments be administered in keeping with God's Word. It is not necessary that human traditions or rites and ceremonies, instituted by men, should be alike everywhere. It is as Paul says in Ephesians 4:4–5: "There is one body and one Spirit, just as you were called to the one hope that belongs to your call, one Lord, one faith, one baptism."[9]

John Calvin likewise should be perceived in this stream of interpretation as an advocate of the church's unity. He is very emphatic about it in his *Institutes:*

> For unless we are united with all the other members under Christ our Head, we can have no hope of the future inheritance. Therefore the Church is called catholic or universal; because there could not be two or three churches, without Christ being divided, which is impossible. But all the elect of God are so connected with each other in Christ, that as they depend on one head, so they grow up together as into one body, compacted together like members of the same body; being made truly one, as living by one faith, hope, and charity, through the same Divine Spirit, being called not only to the same inheritance of eternal life, but also to a participation of one God and Christ.[10]

Calvin's inclination was toward an ecumenical perspective from the outset, but through his contacts with Martin Bucer in Strasburg, his interest in church unity deepened. "Calvin never for a moment ceased to view the Church in its totality, and his ecumenicity took root in the churches organized under his influence, resulting in a strong feeling of unity and an active intercourse between them."[11]

Reformed teaching that bears the unmistakable imprint of Calvin continues the insistence on the church's unity. The Reformed confessions continue this imprint—Second Helvetic (1566), Gallican (1559), Scots (1560), Belgic (1560), and The Heidelberg Catechism (1562).

When a twentieth-century Christian looks back to the sixteenth-century arena with the unity theme as the guiding map, it is truly remarkable how distant is the stereotype of individualistic Protestantism. The Reformers did not turn their backs on the affirmation of the Roman Catholic Church. They passionately affirmed the communion of saints and greatly longed for unity. Not only Luther and Calvin can be studied from this perspective; others, too, can be so viewed— Zwingli, Oecolampadius, Melanchthon, Bucer, Beza, Knox, and leading Anglican bishops of the sixteenth and seventeenth centuries.

Later Movements of Evangelical Renewal

In the post-Reformation era, a number of movements that served to breathe new life into the life stream of the people of God can be identified and studied. Evangelical Christians in the latter decades of the twentieth century would reap rich benefits by overcoming an ahistorical, sectarian mentality and getting in touch with those historical movements that have nurtured the evangelical spirit. The unity of the body has frequently surfaced as integral to a conception of the church that is both compatible with and faithful to the New Testament picture.

Pietism

Late seventeenth-century and early eighteenth-century Pietism in Germany, as well as other expressions of the Pietist heritage, have often been charged with excessive subjectivism and runaway individualism. That Pietism was historically concerned with the renewal of spiritual fervor and devotion for individual persons is indisputable. This renewal, however, was set within the context and the framework of the larger church. In pristine Pietism, there was no intention of schism from the visible company of the church. The conventicles in the early years of Pietism were never designed to be enclaves of devotion that should have a separate existence from the larger congregation nor from the still larger body of the church. Their thrust was to serve as a renewing movement within the larger church, energizing the people of God toward the goal of a "holy life" that would match a "holy doctrine."

Both Philipp Jacob Spener and August Hermann Francke were open to other Christian traditions. In Berlin, Spener served as a mediator between Lutheran and Reformed churches; he possessed a keen longing for harmony and unity within the body of Christ. Francke actually hoped for the establishment of a universal seminary where pastors and priests of diverse confessions would prepare for service within their own church bodies but with a substantial accent on "true

Christianity." Martin Schmidt has given a detailed insight into
Francke's far-reaching vision:

> But Francke looked far beyond the western world. In Heinrich
> Milde he found a young translator who took the principal share
> in rendering the Bible into Russian, Czech, and Polish, and also
> the translation of Arndt's *True Christianity* into Russian. With the
> help of Count Wreech, Francke started work at Tobolsk in
> Siberia among German prisoners captured in the Northern War
> (i.e. the war between Sweden and Russia, 1700–1721), and
> thereafter in the German Lutheran congregations in Russia. In
> every possible way, but particularly through travellers, ambassa-
> dors, officers, merchants, and scholars, he propagated the
> Pietism of Halle, which in this way was spread to southeast
> Europe and Scandinavia, to Russia and Central Asia, to England
> and North America. All this was carefully planned and deliber-
> ately undertaken. Yet it all seemed to happen with the inevitabil-
> ity of a dynamic movement, living by its claim to be the bearer of
> true Christianity in the contemporary world. The work was car-
> ried out by means of a widely extended network of correspon-
> dence, carefully developed and skillfully organized, which in its
> purpose and range recalls the great period of ecumenical activity
> in the hands of such men as Luther, Bucer, and Calvin.[12]

Puritanism

Puritanism, as well as Pietism, has sometimes been viewed as
a sectarian, divisive, unecumenical movement. There is ample
evidence, however, that many Puritans nourished a longing
for Christian unity. John Bunyan was one of these ecumeni-
cally minded churchmen. As a Baptist pastor in Bedford, he
practiced an open-membership policy, defending his practices
against the criticism of colleagues in a book published in 1673
entitled *Differences in Judgment About Water Baptism No Bar to
Communion*. He wrote:

> All I say is that the Church of Christ hath not warrant to keep out
> of their communion the Christian that is discovered to be a visible
> saint by the Word, the Christian that walketh according to his
> light with God. . . . Christ, not Baptism, is the way to the sheep-
> fold.[13]

Richard Baxter was another ardent spokesman for Christian unity. His clear statement in *The Reformed Pastor* is a model of an abiding commitment to oneness in Christ:

> I would . . . recommend to all my brethren, as the most necessary thing to the Church's peace, that they unite in necessary truths, and bear with one another in things that may be borne with; and do not make a larger creed and more necessaries than God hath done. . . . He that shall live to that happy time when God will heal His broken Churches, will see all this that I am pleading for reduced to practice, and this moderation take the place of the new-dividing seal, and the doctrine of the sufficiency of Scripture established; and all men's confessions and comments valued only as subservient helps, and not made the test of church communion, any further than they are the same with Scripture.[14]

Moravianism

The passion of Count Nicolaus Ludwig von Zinzendorf, leader of the eighteenth-century Moravians, for church unity has been amply documented, especially in the impressive work by A. J. Lewis, *Zinzendorf, the Ecumenical Pioneer: A Study in the Moravian Contribution to Christian Mission and Unity.* Zinzendorf may have been the first Christian personage in modern times to use the word *oikoumene* as meaning "the worldwide church." He personally felt the scandal of disunity within the Christian church, but he nevertheless respected the denominations, each one bearing a "school of wisdom" and having a distinctive contribution to make to the whole body of Christ. One of the reports about his concern for oneness concerns correspondence that he carried on with the pope about the vision of a hymnal that could be used by all Christians in their common worship of God.

Zinzendorf's vision of unity was related to his passionate devotion to the spread of the global Christian mission.

> Zinzendorf hoped beyond hope that the unity of the churches he had preached for a life-time would come in embryo on the mission field and flower across the whole of Christendom. Denominationalism on the mission field had no place in his calculations.

"In Europe," he said, "our divisions are rooted in necessity and love, but there is no sense, let alone Christianity, in carting the stuff to America." "It pains me," he wrote, "to see people polishing up the Churches again for the heathen and asking them to which of the Christian Denominations they belong." "You must not enrol your converts as members of the Moravian Church," he instructed the missionaries, "you must be content to enrol them as Christians."[15]

Methodism

The Methodist tradition can also be seen in connection with its ecumenical vision. John Wesley wrote and spoke often of the universal church and the need for overcoming the divisions within the body.

Would to God that all party names and unscriptural phrases and forms which have divided the Christian world were forgot, and that we might all agree to sit down together, as humble, loving disciples, at the feet of our common Master, to hear His word, to imbibe His Spirit, and to transcribe His life on our own.
'And if ye salute your friends only' (Matthew 5:47): Our Lord probably glances at those prejudices, which different sects had against each other, and intimates, that he would not have his followers imbibe that narrow spirit. Would to God this had been more attended to among the unhappy divisions and subdivisions, into which the Church has been crumbled! And that we might at least advance so far, as cordially to embrace our brethren in Christ, of whatever party or denomination they are![16]

Wesley was insistent that unity among Christians constituted the very essence of the church and that the mission of the church was severely hindered by disunity and division.

These are but a few glimpses of evangelical roots drawn primarily from the sixteenth, seventeenth, and eighteenth centuries. The Evangelical Alliance constituted in London in 1846 serves as a prime example of Christian unity drawn from the nineteenth century, and there are many others that could be included. As evangelical Christians today consider the character of the traditions that have shaped their past, it is imperative that they look for ecumenical links. A number of questions call for responses:

What *was* the fully-orbed teaching of the Reformation and the post-Reformation renewal movements about the church? What *was* said about the unity and the universality of the church by Luther, Calvin, Zwingli, Oecolampadius, Bucer, Melanchthon, Knox, and Cranmer? By Spener, Francke, Labadie, Zinzendorf, Baxter, Bunyan, Owen, Mather, Edwards, Wesley, and a host of others who helped form the foundations of evangelical Christianity?

Why have evangelicals frequently bypassed the note of the unity of the body in their own particular traditions in support of separation, isolation, and division?

Why have evangelicals often been reluctant to recognize the work of God in traditions other than their own? Why have they often maintained a standoffishness in inter-church relationships?

Unity Made Visible and Concrete

The unity that marks the nature of the church has often been characterized as being entirely a matter of the spirit. The whole collection of biblical images about the church and all references to unity have sometimes been interpreted as an invisible, incorporeal reality, "known only to God." Many evangelical Christians have accepted this perspective, thereby relieving them of a sense of pain and frustration at the divisions and separations that are evident throughout the church today.

Evangelicals are being summoned in these latter years of the twentieth century to refuse to settle for these mere spiritualized concepts of church unity and to affirm the conviction that unity in Christ demands visible and concrete expression. The precedents for visibility and concreteness are significant in resisting Docetism. Jesus Christ, the living Word of God, became flesh and blood. The church, too, became flesh and blood in time and space—in Corinth, in Rome, in Philippi, in Thessalonica, in Galatia, and elsewhere throughout the first-century world.

So also with the persistent and pressing theme of church unity. Consigned to the invisible world, the world of spirit and the abstract, it costs no one anything. This perspective maintains that this unity cannot be observed by real human eyes. This, however, is to deny a basic facet of the whole thing. The truth is that unity is not only a gift; it is also an assignment. It is both gift and demand. It is at the same time the gift of God and the will of God. Unity is a goal to be cultivated. It is an intention to be constantly bathed in sincere prayer and sought with passion.

That many evangelicals are taking seriously the call to cultivate unity visibly and concretely has become increasingly evident. One of these evidences is the growing number of occasions and events in which evangelicals are encountering one another and searching for a common witness. The 1973 Chicago Declaration of Evangelical Social Concern was one such concrete expression. On that occasion about fifty persons convened in Chicago to discuss their common convictions about the social message of the church, and issued a pastoral letter to the larger evangelical community.[17] They set an evangelical agenda for the consideration of such sobering issues as racism, social injustice, materialism, sex discrimination, war, and violence. A number of spinoffs from that event developed, the most determined being a cultivation of Christian feminism that demands recognition.

Another concrete expression was the gathering of nearly fifty scholars and students in May, 1977, at a Roman Catholic retreat center just outside Chicago to draft the Chicago Call. The manifesto appealed to evangelicals everywhere to seek maturation as Christians and abandon narrow "sectarian mentality."

The most renowned occasion in recent times, that brought evangelicals together, however, was the International Congress on World Evangelization in Lausanne, Switzerland, in 1974. Over twenty-five hundred participants shared in the conference, augmented by fifteen hundred observers. One hundred and fifty countries were represented, including a substantial number from the third world.[18]

Many of the papers and speeches at the congress, as well as the sectional reports and parts of the covenant that were adopted called evangelicals to a renewed and vigorous quest for church unity. It should be noted that about sixty percent of the churches represented at the congress were at the same time members of the World Council of Churches.[19]

That evangelicals are more and more involved in the ecumenical conciliar movement is a further indication of visible and concrete expression. An increasing number of evangelical bodies have affiliated with the World Council of Churches, including many from third world countries. Evangelical consultants are frequently invited to the World Council events. One observer at the Nairobi Assembly in 1975 was so impressed with the seriousness of discussion on evangelism that he commented, "it is probably true that the World Council of Churches is more open to evangelical input today than in the past." The same observer asserted that "there are millions of evangelicals who are in denominations that belong to the WCC. A significant number of delegates at Nairobi applied the term evangelical to themselves and a still larger number reflected a generally evangelical orientation."[20]

Another commentator, John H. Kromminga, pointed out that the Lausanne Congress had a considerable effect on the Nairobi Assembly. Section I, "Confessing Christ Today," was profoundly influenced by evangelical input.[21]

Evangelicals have also been engaged in dialog in the United States with representatives of the National Council of Churches. A two-day consultation in March, 1975, brought together twenty-five "evangelical" and "ecumenical" Protestants around the theme, "Evangelism and Social Justice." There was general agreement that Christians of differing traditions can cooperate on such issues as "world hunger and the developing of new Christian life styles in a declining economy."[22]

Still another visible and concrete expression can be identified in relation to the bilateral conversations that have taken place in recent years by officially appointed representatives of two churches, two traditions, or two confessional families—the purposes ranging from the promotion of mutual understanding to achieving full fellowship. Examples of these bilaterals include the following bodies: Baptist/Reformed; Lutheran/Anglican; Catholic/Pentecostal; Evangelical/Catholic. An Evangelical/Roman Catholic Dialogue on Mission took place in Venice in April, 1977. The Vatican Secretariat for Christian Unity appointed eight members, and eight evangelicals were constituted as an *ad hoc* international group, including Bishop Donald Cameron of Australia, Peter Beyerhaus of Tübingen, David Hubbard of Fuller Seminary, and John R.W. Stott of London. Dr. Stott's description of the interchange is noteworthy:

> Although we came together with some fears and suspicions of one another, soon the caricatures were discarded, and through patient listening we came to know, respect, and love one another in the Holy Spirit. We spent one evening sharing our personal experiences of Jesus Christ and our testimonies to him, and we rejoiced to recognize God's grace in one another . . .

> We hope to meet again and to tackle in greater depth some of the main issues that still divide us. I find myself hoping and praying that evangelicals worldwide will take more initiatives to develop friendly conversations with Roman Catholics based on common Bible study. It would be tragic indeed if God's purpose of reformation were frustrated by our evangelical stand-offishness. One of the Nottingham Congress's final "Declarations of Intent" concerned Roman Catholics and said: "We renew our commitment to seek with them the truth of God and the unity he wills, in obedience to our common Lord on the basis of Scripture."[23]

As evangelical Christians today ponder the necessity of cultivating unity and working toward its realization, several questions press for open and frank responses:

How can the Lausanne stream in modern ecumenism

and the Geneva stream complement each other? Are there common areas of dialog and service that can be developed?

How can such diverse ecumenical bodies as the National Association of Evangelicals and the National Council of Churches increase contacts, working toward common service and mission? Is it possible even to envision an eventual merger of these two Christian bodies?

Is it feasible for evangelicals to reach out responsibly in both directions and expand dialog and common social service—to more fundamentalist groups on the right and to more liberal groups on the left? How much is achievable?

How much do Christians of varied and distinct traditions intercede for one another?

How can diverse ministerial bodies and diverse church bodies in metropolitan America begin to talk with each other?

Evangelical and Ecumenical

I believe the time has come for all the stops to be pulled out in the contemporary quest for church unity. The development of encounter and cooperation within Christ's church should be warmly embraced. Evangelicals should now be encouraged to cultivate increased awareness, increased discussion, and increased cooperation both within and without their respective traditions, earnestly seeking common areas of agreement and understanding. Some of the implications are translatable into the following challenges:

It means setting aside stereotypes, labels, and quick judgments, accepting the fact that we are not dealing with monolithic structures or entities, but with variegated perspectives within a common Christian history.

It means affirming the realization that no single church body and no single tradition has the foreclosed corner on Christian truth.

It means humbly supporting the belief that evangelicals need the whole church in their pilgrimage toward maturation, and at the same time unashamedly maintaining that the whole church needs the evangelical witness in order for there to be a balanced perspective.

It means resisting the false dichotomy between evangelical on the one hand and ecumenical on the other, insisting rather that it is possible to be both passionately evangelical and, simultaneously, passionately ecumenical.

It means rejecting the false dichotomy between evangelism and social justice, believing rather that both are demanded in faithfulness and obedience to the biblical message.

It means accepting the premise that church unity is a goal toward which we earnestly strive and pray. The Week of Prayer for Christian Unity should be recorded on every evangelical church calendar.

It means the consideration of possible mergers by denominational bodies and possible union of local congregations under the guidance of the Holy Spirit and responsible churchmanship.

It means joining together in common cause with all Christians to defend the social and economic rights of the poor and the oppressed.

It means avoiding doctrinal indifferentism and a false irenicism and encouraging evangelicals to cultivate increased discussion and cooperation.[24]

It means being open to dialog about matters of common worship and practice—a fixed date for Easter, liturgy orders, the sacraments.

It means exploring in communities across the country and across the world concrete and visible ways of working together in meeting the needs of the community, searching the Scriptures together, worshipping together, praying together, facing the future together.

Hear the word of the Lord:

There is one body and one Spirit, just as you were called to the one hope that belongs to your call, one Lord, one faith, one baptism, one God and Father of us all, who is above all and through all and in all.

—Ephesians 4:4-6

Notes

1. "Lausanne Covenant" (Lausanne, Switzerland: International Congress on World Evangelization), Clause 7.

2. Eduard Schweizer, *The Church As the Body of Christ* (Richmond: John Knox Press, 1964), p. 63.

3. Dietrich Bonhoeffer, *Life Together* (New York: Harper and Brothers, 1954), p. 21.

4. Paul Minear, *Images of the Church in the New Testament* (Philadelphia: Westminster Press, 1960).

5. John T. McNeill, *Unitive Protestantism: The Ecumenical Spirit and Its Persistent Expression* (Richmond: John Knox Press, 1964), p. 15.

6. Ibid., p. 16.

7. William G. Rusch, "Lutheran Views on Church Unity," *Mid-Stream* 16, no. 3 (July 1977): 329.

8. Martin Luther, *Luther's Works;* 7th ed. (Weimar: n.p.), p. 219.

9. Theodore G. Tappert, ed., *The Book of Concord* (Philadelphia: Fortress Press, 1976), p. 32.

10. John Calvin, *Institutes of the Christian Religion,* trans. John Allen, Volume II, 7th ed. (Philadelphia: Presbyterian Board of Christian Education, 1936), p. 271.

11. Ruth Rouse and Stephen Neill, eds., *A History of the Ecumenical Movement, 1517–1948* (Philadelphia: Westminster Press, 1967), p. 52.

12. Ibid., pp. 100–01.

13. Robert G. Torbet, *Ecumenism . . . Free Church Dilemma* (Valley Forge: Judson Press, 1968), p. 55.

14. Quoted in Donald Bloesch, *The Evangelical Renaissance* (Grand Rapids: Eerdmans, 1973), p. 121.

15. A.J. Lewis, *Zinzendorf, the Ecumenical Pioneer: A Study in the Moravian Contribution to Christian Mission and Unity* (Philadelphia: Westminster Press, 1962), p. 95.

16. Colin W. Williams, *John Wesley's Theology Today* (New York: Abingdon Press, 1960), p. 14.

17. See Ronald J. Sider, ed., *The Chicago Declaration* (Carol Stream, Ill.: Creation House, 1974).

18. See C. Rene Padilla, ed. *The New Face of Evangelicalism* (Downers Grove, Ill.: InterVarsity Press, 1976).

19. Cornish Rogers, "World Council Assembly: A Sober Celebration," *Christian Century* 92, no. 41 (10 December 1975): 1123.

20. Ronald J. Sider, "Evangelicals and the World Council of Churches," *Engage/Social Action* (February/March 1976): 44.

21. "Evangelical Influence on the Ecumenical Movement," *Calvin Theological Journal* (November 1976): 162.

22. *Christian Century* (9 April 1975): 351.

23. *Christianity Today* (12 August 1977): 1175.

24. See "The Chicago Call," section on "Church Unity."

III. Responses

11. Reservations about Catholic Renewal in Evangelicalism

by

DAVID F. WELLS

David F. Wells is Professor of Church History and History of Christian Thought at Trinity Evangelical Divinity School. He earned the Ph.D. at the University of London and is the author of several books including Revolution in Rome *(Downers Grove: InterVarsity Press, 1972) and* Search For Salvation *(Downers Grove: InterVarsity Press, 1978).*

The renewal of catholic spirituality within evangelicalism needs to be considered from two angles. From one point of view it is a rejection of the cultic aspects of evangelicalism; from another, it is the positive attempt to form an amalgam between an evangelical "heart piety" and a more broadly based and ecclesiastically centered tradition. With the first I am more than sympathetic, but with the second I am less than enthusiastic.

It goes without saying that that elusive balance between simplicity and profundity, which is the genius of authentic biblical faith, has been disturbed in our time. Evangelical faith to be sure, has hardly ever run the risk of being co-opted by the intellectuals, but it is consistently vulnerable to a degeneration at the point of its simplicity. When divorced from profundity, simplicity becomes superficiality. We have it in the evangelical church and those evangelicals who refuse to allow that this is anything more than a masquerade of genuine faith are right.

How frequently, for example, has the kingdom of God been transformed into show business! We have our rhinestone evangelists and our gold-plated preachers, practitioners of electronic coquetry who emit velvety comfort and dispense smooth promises. Theirs is a world of Cadillacs and sequins, of slick PR men, easy slogans, TV make-up, and kindergarten Christianity. The idols in this empty world are its muscled Jocks for Jesus. Its leaders are those who have a pipeline to loose money. Given this fabric of fantasy, the fame of a converted star, any star, can be shared vicariously by the psychologically deprived. It is a world that creates instant heroes (and abandons them as rapidly), that dresses up piety in mascara, agonizing problems in simple solutions (Praise the Lord!), and the faith of the ages in little-minded conformity and personal eccentricity (Praise the Lord!). It also propels nice housewives like Marabel Morgan to national prominence as its most profound and articulate theologians. Yes, there is something wrong with all of this, but I cannot be persuaded that we would be substantially better off venerating Catholic saints than pretty starlets, or that sober-faced genuflectors and swingers of incense are much to be preferred to the vacant worshippers some of our churches are creating. This may be a time of small happenings, of Pygmy spirituality, but a mass pilgrimage into the world of Anglo-Catholicism is not, with all due respect, what we need right now. Indeed, it is not what we need at any time.

Yet this is precisely what some of those at the Chicago Call considered to be evangelicalism's last hope, without which profundity would be forever lost and shallow superficiality forever present. Indeed, the reporter for *Newsweek* (May 23, 1977, p. 6) clearly detected among the delegates a deep dissatisfaction with the "sectarian" mentality in evangelicalism as seen in its heavy emphasis on personal conversion, its "low regard for reason and high tolerance for boisterous Biblicism," its "anarchic individualism," and its "long sermons and emotional hymns." As an antidote to all of this, he heard the delegates hankering after an authoritarian church, a dependence on tradition, liturgical worship which would relegate the sermon to the periphery, and, in his opinion, "an almost Catholic view of baptism and the Lord's Supper." He had no difficulty in concluding, therefore, that the Callers had given "their favorable nod toward Catholicism" and in some cases were trying to return to "pre-Reformation Catholic understandings of the faith."

In a number of instances, voting over certain phrases showed that those favoring a Pre-Reformation approach similar to the Anglo-Catholic were just shy of a majority.[1] Consequently, others whose roots were explicitly reformational were able to blunt and modify this yearning for a type of spirituality that has more often than not located itself at a safe and respectable distance from evangelicalism. The Call taken as a whole, however, is not entirely free of the grey and shadowy presence of a Catholic outlook. It is, as a result, made up of large patches of ambiguity loosely stitched together with indignation. The indignation, the object of which is the degenerative side of evangelicalism, I understand; the ambiguity, which is intended as a remedy for the various maladies that are diagnosed, leaves me rather baffled. There are three subjects in particular that regularly produce gastric protestations as I try to swallow the Chicago Call.

First, the statement on Scripture is curiously muted and ill-designed. There were in fact two groups around whose strong feelings the rest of the Callers tried to negotiate. On the one side amongst some of the non-Anglo-Catholics there was considerable resistance to the idea of inerrancy. Instead the word *infallible* was used. But in what sense? Even a novice knows that it can be frustratingly elastic in the hands of some people. Was it being so used here? We really do not know

This, however, was not the line of the more traditionally minded who have generally had a high regard for the inspiration of Scripture. Like their full-blown Roman Catholic brethren, however, they have a notable tendency to subjugate it hermeneutically to the teaching of the church and this aspect, like the inerrancy question, is handled with the utmost delicacy in the Call. It is confessed that "the fullness of our Christian heritage" has been lost—a heritage against which Scripture is to be understood; it is deplored that Scripture is not interpreted "with respect for the historic understanding of the church"; it is urged that confessions from the past "should serve as a guide for the interpretation of Scripture"; and our failure to recognize the authority of the church in general is deplored. At the same time, to protect other sensitivities, the Callers inserted ringing affirmations to the effect that confessional authority is in fact subject to biblical authority and that the church must be reformed by the Scriptures.

This, however, merely lays bare the heart of the problem while leaving the false impression that the problem has been solved. What are we to do if the Scriptures contradict the confessions? Is the biblical Word to be subject to the creedal declarations? The Call affirms that it is not. Then if the creeds and confessions are to be judged in the light of Scripture, each believer exercising his priestly obligation of interpretation in concert with the leading of the Spirit, how is this different from the "tendency toward individualistic interpretation" that is deplored? The Call does not tell us and that is the problem that still has to be addressed.

Only those who are historical neophytes would imagine that the thousands of creeds and confessions which are extant represent a solid and undivided testimony as to the meaning of Scripture; only those who are naive would be unable to see that creeds and confessions are all culturally bound in their perception of truth and therefore prone to error. Are we, for example, really to commit ourselves to the Origenist notion of the Son's eternal generation implicit in Nicea's phrases "God from God, light from light, true God from true God"? And what about Chalcedon's benediction on the title of *theotokos* for Mary, which, of course, has passed into popular piety as "Mother of God"? The Fourth Lateran Council endorsed the Cyprianic dictum that outside the Church, *nulla salus* (no salvation). Should Scripture be read in the light of this, too? The Lutherans in their Augsburg Confession declared the truth of consubstantiation and in the Marburg Articles that of baptismal regeneration. The framers of the Westminster Confession a little later let it be known that the pope was the antichrist. Are these affirmations to guide us in our reading of the biblical Word? I take it that those who wish to subject the interpretation of Scripture to the (undefined) mind of the church are obliged to be rather selective about doing it, while those who are evangelical enough to resist this approach are simply affirming that Christians in their work of interpretation should not be parochial. That is so obvious one wonders whether it was worth saying.

What I in fact suspect is that evangelical Anglo-Catholics will opt for a *practical* rather than a theoretical answer to this problem. While affirming the full inspiration of the written Scriptures, they will relegate the sermon to the periphery of worship and simply graft their piety onto a church often functioning without conscious relation to the Word. That, in my opinion, will be to repeat the very error that has brought us to the present state of weakness in the church.

For oddly enough, this is precisely what has happened in many fundamentalist-evangelical churches, even in some of those that would go to the stake for inerrancy. In practice they, too, doff their hats to Scripture and then look the other way. Expository preaching, alive with the recreative power of God is a rare commodity today; almost as rare, indeed, as rain was in the days of Elijah. The majority of evangelical sermons which one hears are simply a mirror of the preacher's consciousness; what he practises in the pulpit is dutifully copied in the pew. Scripture is greatly honored, little heard, and even less obeyed. Judged by the phenomena of evangelical life, a stranger might never guess that originally it grew out of the conviction that the knowledge of God is correlative with his written Word in Scripture and the loss of the one results in the loss of the other. A faded knowledge of God inevitably produces uncertainty about the meaning of Scripture. The problem of "individualistic interpretations" is not, in my judgment, an historical, still less an ecclesiastical problem, but fundamentally one of malformed spirituality. The malady the Call diagnosed, it has not even begun to remedy.

The second area of difficulty for me in the Call concerns the sacraments. The Callers announce their distress both over the "sacramental poverty" of our churches and our failure "to appreciate the sacramental nature of God's activity." A net of condemnation so broad—however loosely it is thrown into the river—is bound to snag a few fishes. If we plead guilty to the charges, however, we might be wise to hesitate before swallowing the remedy without careful thought. It comes, not from Scripture, but mostly from the Greek and Russian Orthodox churches.

The definition that the Call assumes of a sacrament is not the traditional one of an outward and visible sign of an inward and invisible grace. Rather, a sacrament is anything material that becomes a vehicle of the Spirit. It is for this reason that it speaks of creation, the Incarnation, and human life as sacramental. In different ways, the Spirit utilizes matter to point us to the life and activity of God. Almost to the letter, however, this corresponds to the teaching found in the fathers of the Eastern church, such as Dionysius the Pseudo-Areopagite, John Chrysostom, and John of Damascus—as well as later theologians like Joasaph, Metropolitan of Ephesus.

It is this conception that has found its way into Russian Orthodoxy and has also become the basis of all representational art in that tradition. The theory is that the material body of Jesus is the image, icon, or representation of God. As such it exemplifies, in its glorifying of God, the original purpose for which the creation was brought forth. The Incarnation, in which we see splendor in the ordinary, is, therefore, sacramental and what applies to Jesus' body also applies to icons in the church. In them, too, there is splendor in the ordinary as the Spirit of God redeems their materiality to praise God. Nicholas Zernov picks up this theme accordingly:

> Icons were for the Russians not merely paintings. They were dynamic manifestations of man's spiritual power to redeem creation through beauty and art. The colours and lines of the icons were not meant to imitate nature; the artists aimed at demonstrating that men, animals, and plants, and the whole cosmos, could be rescued from their present state of degradation and restored to their proper "Image." The icons were pledges of the coming victory of a redeemed creation over the fallen one. . . The artistic perfection of an icon was not only a reflection of the celestial glory—it was a concrete example of matter restored to its original harmony and beauty, and serving as a vehicle of the Spirit. The icons were part of the transfigured cosmos.[2]

The Callers laid the foundation for the acceptance of these and many other aspects of religious life from the Eastern churches. That they failed to draw out the conclusions more clearly is unfortunate because the underlying assumptions may now go undetected.

This drift toward the Eastern churches was done in the name of "many of the Fathers" and, the Call erroneously adds, the "Reformers." Had it mentioned only the early Greek Fathers it would have been on solid historical ground; certainly it is a mistake to have overlooked the pioneering work of Augustine, for he rightly insisted that a sacrament must be sanctioned by the words of Christ.

The three conditions under which we may speak of something as being a sacrament or of being sacramental are that Christ established it as such, that he commanded its continuing observance in the church, and that it symbolizes God's saving acts as these are proclaimed in the gospel. This is the definition the New Testament assumes; it is not, unfortunately, the definition which the Callers have assumed. For them, sacramental significance is infused into the whole of the created order; for Christ, what is sacramental are the two sacraments that he instituted and commanded the church to observe. These are

Baptism and the Lord's Supper. It is these that the early church observed in conjunction with its preaching of the gospel. It is only these that it ever observed or recognized. Forgive me for asking, then, but on what grounds do the Callers prescribe as sacramental what the church's head, our Lord Jesus Christ, declined to do?

Third, I am unsatisfied with the Call's statement on salvation, which is imprecise enough to give comfort both to Anglo-Catholics and liberation theology.

With respect to this imprecision we might reflect, for example, on the sentence calling us "to participate fully in God's saving activity through work and prayer." I may not have understood the Call aright, but at present I see only three possible interpretations. The simplest meaning is that the Callers think evangelicals are somewhat slothful. Because we neither work nor pray enough, we show insufficient signs of being saved. We are soteriologically half-baked, so this exhortation is essentially a moral one. The way this sentence is worded, however, leads me to think that a moral interpretation is not what the Callers intended. The thought seems to be that of working *in* salvation to remedy a deficiency, rather than working *out* a salvation already fully possessed. I am inclined to think, then, that we should opt for a theological interpretation.

The Call opens with the charge that evangelicals are "blind to the work of God in others" and later we hear the exhortation to explore "devotional practice in all traditions within the church [Marian devotion as well?] in order to deepen our relationship both with Christ and with other Christians." The reason that we are half-saved, perhaps, is that we are disconnected from all of those other rites, theologies, and traditions that contain that part of salvation we are missing. The World Council of Churches has been saying this for years. Does this sentence exhort us to listen to that charge?

Then again, this might not be what the Callers had in mind. If we exegete the sentence by accenting the word *through*, we can elicit yet another meaning. God saves people *through* work and prayer, so it is through work and prayer that we are saved.

This, however, seems to be cut from the same cloth that the first century Judaizers used, and I was under the impression that Paul was not well pleased with their teaching, but perhaps I am wrong.

The main difficulty I have and where I find this section of the Call misleading is in its concept of "holistic salvation." This notion comes to resemble a magician's hat out of which the Callers, at the stroke of their wand, can produce almost anything. Under the rubric of salvation appear physical and emotional healing, "justice for the oppressed and disinherited," and stewardship "of the natural world." That the church should show compassion to the poor, the needy, the suffering, and that the church should be ecologically responsible is not in question. Social and ecological responsibility, however, are the *consequences* of salvation, not its *substance*. The failure to make this distinciton in the Call is, I believe, unfortunate.

It is, of course, true that in the Old Testament, salvation is often conceived in starkly physical terms. The terminology it uses—*hayah, yasha', ga'a', padah kōpher*—frequently suggests this. To be saved meant being kept alive, preserved, being freed to develop or being ransomed, body for body. More often than not, people were saved from enemies, disease, pestilence, castastrophe, and disorder. They were also saved from sin and God's judgment, but the spiritual aspect was by no means the exclusive one. Were we living solely with the Old Testament, there might be justification for saying that God saves people partly by reversing injustice and alleviating social distress; there is no justification for so thinking once the New Testament is allowed its rightful place in our theology.

In the New Testament, almost without exception, the doctrine of salvation is internalized and spiritualized. Man is saved from enemies who are spiritual rather than physical. It is from the grip of evil powers, the guilt and condemnation of sin, the old aeon, the old state, the old man, and the old fears that we are saved. This is true of the appearance of *sōzo* in all three tenses. Whether we are thinking of salvation as a past event in justification, a present experience in sanctification, or a future hope in glorification, the enemies, almost invariably, are spiritual. This is why the New Testament writers developed the doctrine of salvation under terms such as grace, faith, regeneration, justification, adoption, union with Christ, conversion, and sanctification. These locate the saving activity of God in the soul of man through the death of Christ; whatever ethical and political consequences flow from this divine work are its *results,* not its substance.

The movement from an Old to a New Testament view can be seen quite plainly in the way that the Bible treats the theme of Exodus. The original Exodus was historical. It was a deliverance that was outward, national, and starkly physical. In the prophetic interpretation of this event, however, a change in the understanding of deliverance begins to be evident. The first Exodus comes to be seen merely as a foreshadowing of a greater Exodus that God will accomplish in the future. In the later prophets there are present some spiritual elements in this new cycle of captivity, release, and divine succor in the wilderness (Isa. 51:10,11; 52:12; 40:3; 48:21). Indeed, one of the best known Isaianic passages— "How beautiful upon the mountains are the feet of him that bringeth good tidings, That publisheth peace, that bringeth good tidings of good, that publisheth salvation, that saith unto Zion, Thy God reigneth" (52:7, KJV)—is set in the context of the prophet's teaching on the new Exodus (vv. 2–6). The conclusion becomes inescapable. Egypt, as Hosea makes plain (7:16, 9:3, 11:5,11), is the land of sin. It is from the bondage of sin that God is going to liberate his people.

It is this theme that reappears in the New Testament. The hope of deliverance was still present in the hearts of pious Jews (Luke 2:38). The Zealots interpreted this politically, but the New Testament understands it spiritually. There is, indeed, a new and greater Moses (Heb. 3:1–15) and there is, again, a passover lamb (1 Cor. 5:7). Furthermore, there is a fresh and greater deliverance, but it is spiritual rather than physical. The word used to describe this is *redemption (apolytrosis)* and it occurs ten times. Christ the passover Lamb was sacrificed, not to redeem us from political institutions or oppressive circumstances, but from the hosts of wickedness and the wrath of God (cf. Eph. 1:7; Rom. 3:24–26; Heb. 9:15; 1 Cor. 6:19,20; Gal. 3:13). We enter this deliverance, not by marching across the opened sea, still less by routing injustice, but by the exercise of faith. This is the New Testament's liberation theology and what it does to the theme of Exodus, it does to all the other aspects of salvation in the Old Testament.

My contention with respect to the Chicago Call, then, is that in its anxiety to correct a view of salvation that is too "spiritual," it has inadvertently returned to an Old Testament understanding. Justice for the oppressed is considered as it would have been partly in the Old Testament but never is in the New Testament. Contained within an Old Testament understanding, the Callers therefore conclude the section on "holistic salvation" by linking the striving "for justice and liberation for the oppressed" to the ongoing work of salvation that will culminate in a new heaven and earth.

It now becomes plain that under the banner of holistic salvation we might find not only those who through their prayers and works are being saved, but also the liberation theologians who through their efforts to change political systems are also participating in God's salvation. The rubric is broad enough to include incense on the one end and revolution on the other. That I find a trifle discomforting.

The Chicago Call, then, has done much to isolate those aspects of evangelicalism that need to be reformed; I am not sure that what has been proposed by way of a remedy is what is really needed. But that, in a way, points up the real significance of the Call. It is not that the Callers fumbled but that many of them had nowhere to go. Having seen the weaknesses in contemporary evangelicalism, they had no reservoir of evangelical reflection and applied spirituality from which they could draw remedies. That is the reason, I think, that in their search for answers they ranged so widely and so indiscriminately among traditions that are essentially incompatible with evangelical belief. The vacuity of contemporary evangelicalism is inadvertently exposed by the Call at least as much as the deficiencies in its own solution.

Notes

1. I include in this category all those who entertain a Romantic view of the early church and who hold the patristic Fathers in special esteem.

2. Nicholas Zernov, *The Russians and Their Church* (London: Fellowship of St. Alban and St. Sergius, 1945), pp. 107–08.

12. A Roman Catholic Appraisal of the Chicago Call

by

BENEDICT T. VIVIANO, O.P.

*Benedict T. Viviano is a member of the Domini-
can Order and Professor of New Testament at
Aquinas Institute of Theology, Dubuque, Iowa.
He holds the Ph.D. from Duke University and the
Licenciate in Sacred Scripture from the Pontifi-
cal Biblical Commission, Rome. He is the author
of* Study As Worship: Aboth And The New
Testament *(Leiden: Brill, 1978).*

I accepted the initial invitation to the Chicago Call conference because of my respect for the solid achievements of
evangelical Christians on the American scene. The chief glory
of evangelicals I take to be their powerful preaching of Jesus
Christ as the joyful instrument of man's salvation. They have a
wonderful knack of presenting the initial joy of conversion to
Christ, of helping people to an adult decision for Christ. (This
talk of decision has roots in Heidegger and Bultmann as well as
in the Bible and Billy Graham.) They do this by directly ex-
pounding the Scriptures and by concentrating on the person
of Jesus Christ.

As a Roman Catholic priest, teacher, and preacher of the New Testament, I have always tried to learn from evangelicals (and others) how best to preach the Word so that it could be effective in reaching present-day people. I did my basic theology in an ecumenical context in which I was told by Lutherans and Presbyterians that I was an evangelical Catholic. As an active participant in the Catholic biblical renewal, I was early impressed not only by the achievements of Protestant biblical scholarship, but also by the heroic achievement of Karl Barth in attempting to construct a systematic theology for our times on the basis of a careful and thorough utilization of the Bible and the tradition of the church.

It is, moreover, obvious to the observer of the American religious scene that one of the growth points of the various Christian bodies is the evangelical-charismatic wing. Therefore, if one wants to be in touch with what is vital in the churches, one has to be in touch with evangelicals. One may do so on opportunistic grounds, jumping on the bandwagon so to speak, and this represents a clear and present danger for the evangelical movement. Or one may do so because one recognizes the finger of God in evangelical vitality. As the prologue to the Call says: "We recognize with gratitude God's blessing through the evangelical resurgence in the church." And one may add to that the recognition of a certain theological affinity between Roman Catholics and evangelicals, as did the late Gustave Weigel, S. J., long before his motives could be considered suspect.[1]

But evangelicals, no more than anyone else, are not without their defects and needs, which have, I believe, been well pinpointed by the Call. For example, it has always struck me that when it comes to preaching the gospel, Billy Graham is very good. But when it comes to resolving the tensions between science and faith, he is not so successful or satisfying. A tradition, such as my own Dominican Thomistic one, which has a long history of serious efforts to relate the data of revelation to philosophy and science, comes off better in this respect. (I may mention that one of my Dominican professors was R. J. Nogar, author of *The Wisdom of Evolution* and *The Lord of the Absurd*.)

I also feel that my church tradition is strong in communicating a sense of historical continuity with Christians of earlier times, in offering a sober, reverent worship to God, in handing on the basic christological elements of the faith, in teaching our individual and social ethical responsibilities as Christians, and in maintaining a sense of the church as a divine and not merely a human reality, as the body of Christ whose unity must not be rent. If another group of Christians expresses a need in these areas, I feel bound to offer whatever help I can when they ask for it. For these reasons, then, I came to the conference.

What value do I see in the outcome of the conference? It seems to me that there is a twofold value. First, to those outside the evangelical movement it will shatter stereotypes they commonly hold about evangelicals. Speaking for myself, and putting it bluntly, the evangelical had always seemed to be a person who knew and cared little (at least as a Christian) about what happened between the close of the New Testament and his own conversion. He leaped through time as though he were not only born again, but born yesterday. This implied that his grasp of the Scriptures would be timeless, devoid of any sense of the historical setting and conditioning of the events of our salvation or of the words in which it is expressed. Thus, the evangelical, in my stereotype, might have a sense of church history, but of a special sort.

Two models come to mind. The first imagines the past two thousand years of the history of the church as a long, black night punctuated by three momentary flashes of light that were then immediately swallowed by the prevailing darkness. (The flashes were, of course, Jesus, Paul, and Luther.) The second model again imagines the course of church history to be a long night black as pitch, but, in this case, there is always a feeble, flickering candle that lights the way for an elect few: Tertullian and the Montanists, Joachim and Flora and the Albigensians, Jan Hus and the Lollards, Savonarola and

Lefèvre d'Étaples. As the Waldensians say, *"Lux lucet in tenebris."*

When I got to the conference, my stereotypes were shattered. I found myself in the presence of men and women who were steeped in the history of the church. Indeed, moments after I arrived, I was bombarded by someone with questions and information about Pauline scholars of the Italian Renaissance. To be sure, our evaluations of historical events did not always coincide.

One of my favorite incidents at the conference came during a dispute over the wording of a sentence in the "Historic Roots and Continuity" article of the Call: "It [an evangelical impulse] flowers in the biblical fidelity of the Protestant Reformers and the ethical earnestness of the Radical Reformation." Someone suggested that there might have been an effort at biblical fidelity within the Church of Rome and not only among the Protestant Reformers. At that, another defended the original wording on the grounds that "Trent was no flower, baby."

I piped up, "Not even a tiny violet?"

"A merest forget-me-not?" impishly added another.

The original wording was retained, despite our gallant efforts. Second, to those within the evangelical movement, I hope the conference will have the value of fulfilling its stated aim. This is to help evangelicals achieve full maturity in the faith by appropriating the fullness of their Christian heritage with its spiritual, theological, liturgical, social, and ecclesiological riches.

Turning now to the statement itself, the obvious general point that needs to be made is that the text is theologically acceptable to me so far as it goes, although it says less than I believe. In its final form the Chicago Call is a consensus statement drafted and signed by people who were coming from very different theological places and is therefore a child of compromise. Everyone lost something in the final struggles over the wording. The wonder is that it was done at all. The ultimate significance of the Call will derive from what I trust is its accurate discernment of problem areas that evangelicals (and others) need to work on.

The sore points in the text, at least those with which I was personally engaged, were the "Call to Biblical Fidelity" and the "Call to Sacramental Integrity." In the committee responsible for the drafting of the statement on Scripture, we decided, after a painful struggle, to sidestep as much as possible the battle over the Bible's inerrancy, as waged by Harold Lindsell. It is not that the members of the committee did not have views on this issue, but that the focus of the conference lay elsewhere.

The conveners of the conference were concerned, so far as I could tell, with the need to interpret Scripture in some continuity with the doctrinal *tradition* of the church, in a word, with the old Reformation problem of Scripture and tradition. Like many continental Protestant theologians, they have come to realize that the Reformation had its exegetical traditions that determined some of its conclusions. It was never a matter of a pure, naked, tradition-free encounter with Scripture. Once this is admitted, attention can shift to further questions, such as which traditions are of ultimate significance, to what extent do they determine our conclusions, how should our teaching develop in continuity with the traditions, and so on.

Because some participants were worried that an explicit endorsement of church exegetical traditions would involve an endorsement of every interpretation of the ancient and medieval church, a prospect repugnant to them, the wording was muted to "with respect for the historic understanding of the church." The example used to turn us away from the word *tradition* was Luke 1:28 where the angel says to Mary, "Hail, O favored one, the Lord is with you!" It was alleged that in the late Middle Ages (at least), this was widely understood to mean the sinlessness of Mary.[2]

My own views of the right relation between Scripture and tradition in the teaching of the church coincide closely with those of Josef Rupert Geiselmann, professor of Catholic theology at Tübingen. His views were not condemned by the Second

Vatican Council, as had been expected. Nor were they unequivocally endorsed. Rather, the Constitution on Divine Revelation was so framed as to allow his views to be taught within the pale of Catholic orthodoxy (cf. *Dei Verbum,* no. 9). Because the conclusion of Geiselmann's fullest statement of his position has never been put into English, I would like to present it here.

> How is the relationship between the Holy Scriptures and the unwritten traditions to be determined? We have, by means of the proof from tradition that there is a contentual sufficiency of Holy Scripture in what concerns faith, and there is a contentual insufficiency in what concerns *mores, consuetudines et leges* (morals, customs and laws) of the church; we have, I say, created the presupposition to be able to answer the question concerning the relationship between Scripture and tradition. As a result, it becomes apparent that this relationship cannot be determined unequivocally.
>
> With respect to faith, the Holy Scripture is contentually sufficient. But, thereby the Sola-Scriptura principle is not yet expressed. For the Holy Scripture is, with respect to the canon of the Scriptures, dependent upon tradition and upon the decision of the church. For it was the Council of Trent which first definitively settled the canon of Holy Scripture. And with respect to the understanding of Holy Scriptures, it needs the clarifying tradition of the Fathers in matters of faith and morals. Tradition in these cases exercises the function of *traditio interpretativa.* Besides, the Holy Scripture is dependent upon the *sensus* which the church maintains and has always maintained, for the explanation of its contents which concern faith and morals.
>
> Here thus holds true with respect to faith the principle: *totum in sacra scriptura et iterum totum in traditione,* completely in Scripture and completely in tradition.
>
> The situation is otherwise with respect to the *mores et consuetudines* of the church. Here Scripture is insufficient and needs tradition for its contentual completion. In these cases, tradition is *traditio constitutiva.*
>
> Here holds true with respect to the *mores et consuetudines* the principle: *partim in sacra scriptura, partim in sine scripto traditionibus,* partly in the Holy Scriptures, partly in tradition.[3]

As for the inerrancy question, the document contents itself with the statement that the Scriptures are "the infallible Word of God" and authoritative in the church. This wording was chosen because it was traditional in Reformation confessional statements and therein the word "infallible" is followed by "in matters of salvation, doctrine, and life." The word was so intended by the authors of this portion of the Call, and it is in this sense that I signed the Call. As so understood, the teaching of the Call on this point does not differ materially from that of the Second Vatican Council (*Dei Verbum*, no. 11). (To be sure, the statement does not of itself preclude a continuing infallible teaching office within the church, however understood, so long as its authority is derived from Scripture, but that is another matter.) My own concern is not so much with inerrancy itself as with the pastoral problem behind it, namely, that many preachers do not really believe in the power or relevance of Scripture but derive the thrust of their message from nonbiblical sources, whether philosophy, or psychology, or some passing fad. Over against this tragic loss of confidence in the *power* and efficacy of Scripture (Heb 4:12; Jer. 23:29) I believe we need to confess, and to demonstrate, our trust in it.

The other article that gave us difficulty, and with the wording of which I was involved, is the "Call to Sacramental Integrity." I only wish to make a single comment on a matter that concerns me. Even though the text was drastically rewritten before reaching its present form, it still expresses a clear call for a sense of the importance of the sacraments. I come from a highly sacramental church and presuppose the value of sacraments. What has been a struggle for me is to find a powerful, practical recognition of the indispensibility of the competent preaching of the Word within my own church. (By now, alas, I know that the preaching is not always very good in Protestant churches either.) The Second Vatican Council has reemphasized the importance of the Word in the ministry of the priest. And Hans Küng in his widely used book on the church certainly emphasizes this aspect of the ministry. Yet John Macquarrie warns us that "The effectiveness of the Church's ministry should not depend, as so often it does in Protestant churches, on the minister's power as a preacher or on any other personal qualities belonging to him. . . . the office itself is the most important thing."[4] I want to agree with Macquarrie, but I have seen men suffer because they have been forced to flatten out their personal qualities and talents to fit into an easily administered pastoral system where they are expected to be as uniform and interchangeable as the consecrated hosts they distribute. This is a tension we will have to live with.

In conclusion, let me say a word about how I believe the Chicago Call has a bearing on the future of Roman Catholic renewal. The church to whose service I have given my life has, as everyone knows, gone through a historical shift of stupendous proportions, virtually unprecedented. In the United States at least, the human and institutional cost of this shift has been high. The temptation to panic has been great, especially in the hysteria of the late sixties. I am sustained in hope by the conviction that the original intention of the men who made the Council, Pope John XXIII, Pope Paul VI, the bishops, and the theologians who worked out the ideas that were embodied in the conciliar decrees, was nothing less than and nothing other than a return to the gospel, an attempt to purify the church in the image of her Lord Jesus Christ who came among us as one poor, humble, wise, and serving. How can God punish us for that? Yet the future of the renewal is at present uncertain.

There is a deep division in the church right now. The men who made the Council were nourished on the biblical theology movement that flourished in a theological climate largely dominated by Karl Barth. But the renewal is taking place right now in a changed atmosphere where the dominating forces derive from Bultmann, Tillich, and worse. The renewal is in danger of degenerating from a return to the gospel to a limp, debilitating form of culture-endorsing humanism. The Hartford Appeal tried to sound a warning a few years ago. The evolution of Hans Küng is symptomatic. He began as a Catholic Barthian who excelled in biblical theology but has drifted through an Idealist phase into a stage where the basic christological faith of the church is muffled. This problem is not confined to the Roman Catholic church.

I signed the Call to express my solidarity with those who are also concerned.

Notes

1. Gustave Weigel, *A Survey of Protestant Theology in our Day* (Westminster, Md.: Newman, 1954).

2. This may be so, but it should be noted that St. Bernard of Clairvaux, Peter Lombard, Alexander of Hales, St. Bonaventure, St. Albert the Great, and St. Thomas Aquinas did not hold this view. (Cf. *Summa theol.* III, q. 27, a. 2.)

3. J.R. Geiselmann, *Die Heilige Schrift und die Tradition* (Freiburg: Herder, 1962; *Quaestiones Disputatae,* no. 18), p. 282 (my translation). The first eighty-three pages of this work have been translated into English as *The Meaning of Tradition* (New York: Herder and Herder, 1966). A more brief statement by Geiselmann of his view may be found in *Christianity Divided,* ed. D.J. Callahan *et al.* (London: Sheed and Ward, 1962).

4. John Macquarrie, *Principles of Christian Theology,* 2nd. ed. (New York: Scribner's, 1977), pp. 436f.

13. An Annotated Bibliography for Further Reading

by

JAN DENNIS

Jan Dennis is an editor at Cornerstone Books, a new division of Good News Publishers. He holds the M.A. degree from Indiana University and is a lecturer in Church History at the Institute of Christian Studies in Chicago.

This annotated bibliography is meant to be *evocative* not *definitive*. Many other books that touch directly or indirectly on the issues raised by the Chicago Call or that inform on the evangelical-historic orthodox approach to the faith could have been included. The books in this listing were chosen because they were thought to exhibit special qualities, such as clarity, vision, sagacity, profundity, provocativeness, comprehensiveness, and incision that others lacked.

Also highly recommended are the writings—too voluminous to be separately listed and annotated—of the Oxford Christians (C. S. Lewis, Dorothy L. Sayers, Charles Williams, J. R. R.

Tolkien, and Owen Barfield). Most of their works are still in print.

Aulen, Gustaf. *Reformation and Catholicity.* E.T. by E. H. Whalstrom. Philadelphia: Muhlenberg Press, 1961. In this important study an eminent Swedish theologian argues persuasively, but not entirely convincingly, that the Reformation spirit preserved biblical and primitive Christianity in its fullness.

Balthasar, Hans Urs von. *Elucidations.* E.T. by J. Riches. London: S.P.C.K., 1975. Compression is a word usually reserved for poetry. But this book packs an extraordinary amount of orthodox theological insight on contemporary issues into its 216 pages.

Berkhouwer, G. C. *Holy Scripture.* E.T. by Jack Rogers. Grand Rapids: Eerdmans, 1975. This book provides a fresh statement on scriptural authority. Some evangelicals may take exception to a few of the views put forward, but the author's basic position stands in continuity with Reformation thought on Scripture.

———. *The Church.* E.T. by J. E. Davison. Grand Rapids: Eerdmans, 1976. This is a creative discussion of the classical marks of the church (unity, holiness, catholicity, apostolicity) from a Reformed perspective. Throughout, dialog is maintained with the best of current Roman Catholic ecclesiological thought.

Bloesch, Donald G. *The Reform of the Church.* Grand Rapids: Eerdmans, 1973. In the face of the growing threat of secularized Christianity, this book presents a thoroughgoing program for renewing and strengthening evangelicalism.

Bouyer, Louis. *The Spirit and Forms of Protestantism.* E.T. by A. V. Littledale. Westminster, Maryland: Newman Press, 1961. This is a pioneering work in which the author, an ex-Lutheran turned Roman Catholic, argues that Reformation truths, such as justification by faith, are fully compatible with Latin theology, properly understood.

Casserley, J. V. Langmead. *Christian Community.* London: Longmans, 1960. The holistic approach to Christianity, which is striking a responsive chord in many today, is masterfully expounded here by a wise theologian.

Chesterton, G. K. *Orthodoxy.* Garden City, N.Y.: Dodd, Mead, 1908. The spectres of unbelief against which Chesterton contended bear an uncanny resemblance to contemporary ones. His profound insights into the faith shame many more recent and systematic apologetical works.

Dennis, Lane T. *A Reason for Hope*. Old Tappan, New Jersey: Fleming H. Revell, 1976. A sense of rootlessness coupled with anxiety about the future characterize much of modern existence. Recapturing a harmonious and ordered *Geist* that replaces secular alienation with the transforming power of the gospel is the theme of this valuable book.

Guitton, Jean. *Great Heresies and Church Councils*. E.T. by F. D. Wieck. New York: Harper and Row, 1965. This most provocative and illuminating book discusses orthodoxy from the viewpoint of a locus of fullness moving through history, always confronting and defeating defective or partial expressions of the faith.

Howard, Thomas. *Splendor in the Ordinary*. Wheaton, Illinois: Tyndale House, 1976. Using Charles Williams's principle of exchanged love, the author brilliantly explores the redemptive possibilities of everyday living. The rooms of a house serve to image different facets of human life and experience.

Hughes, John Jay. *Stewards of the Lord*. London: Sheed and Ward, 1970. The first Anglican priest to be received into the Roman Catholic ministry without reordination thoroughly discusses the insufficiencies of late Medieval Latin thinking on ministry, sacrament, and church, and concludes that only by incorporating legitimate Reformation motifs—without rejecting true Catholic substance—can ministers be full stewards of the Lord.

Knox, Ronald A., and Arnold Lunn. *Difficulties*. London: Eyre and Spottiswoode, 1932. A good part of the appeal of this correspondence between a Catholic and Protestant on areas of disagreement lies in the freshness and immediacy of the participants' views. This is a needful exercise in issues' clarification.

Lackmann, Max. *The Augsburg Confession and Catholic Unity*. E.T. by W. R. Bouman. New York: Herder and Herder, 1963. We are deeply indebted to the author for showing that at the Reformation, Protestants rejected essential dogmas and institutions of the church, while Catholics were unable to formulate the faith in sufficiently evangelical language. Lackmann paves the way for a new and creative approach to ecumenism.

Leech, Kenneth. *Soul Friend*. London: Sheldon Press, 1977. There has long been the need for a source book on Christian spirituality. This book brings together both neglected and standard works on the Christian spiritual tradition and shows how past masters can throw light on the nagging problems of contemporary spirituality.

Mascall, Eric L. *Christ, the Christian and the Church.* London: Longmans, 1967. Starting with the insight that the permanence of Christ's manhood is the foundational principle of Christian theology, the author skillfully explores the consequences for Christianity in the areas of atonement, Baptism, Eucharist, church, prayer, and theology.

———. *Corpus Christi.* London: Longmans, 2nd ed., 1965. This book provides an excellent critical overview of recent developments in both Protestant and Catholic eucharistic theology.

Montgomery, John W. *Ecumenicity, Evangelicals and Rome.* Grand Rapids: Zondervan, 1969. Though encumbered by a surfeit of footnotes and annoying "theology-ese," this book nevertheless clearly defines the limits of agreement and therefore co-operation among evangelical, mainline Protestant, Roman Catholic, and Eastern Orthodox Christians. The high point is a provocative, though problematic, analysis of Eastern Orthodoxy.

Prenter, Regin. *The Word and the Spirit.* E.T. by H. E. Kaasa. Minneapolis: Augsburg, 1965. The tendency of modern Christians to separate God's Word (Christ) from His Holy Spirit is probingly analyzed in a variety of contemporary theological contexts. The book urges maintaining the unity of the work of Word and Spirit.

Pfürtner, Stephen. *Luther and Aquinas on Salvation.* New York: Sheed and Ward, 1965. In examining the controversy between Catholics and Protestants on the doctrine of the Christian's hope and certainty of personal salvation, Fr. Pfürtner discovers much more agreement than had hitherto been found. The book raises the larger question: Have past doctrinal disagreements on other issues been similarly misunderstood by both sides?

Ramsey, A. Michael. *The Gospel and the Catholic Church.* London: Longmans, 1957. The former Archbishop of Canterbury, basing his analysis on Christ's person and work, stresses the need to recognize the mutual interdependence of gospel and church for a full expression of the faith.

Sartory, Thomas. *The Oecumenical Movement and the Unity of the Church.* Oxford: Basil Blackwell, 1963. Despite its pre-Vatican II orientation, this is a very valuable contribution to ecumenical literature because of its systematic and rigorous approach to doctrinal differences.

Tavard, George H. *Holy Writ or Holy Church.* New York: Harper and Brothers, 1969. Recent re-evaluations of the relationship between Scripture and tradition in both Catholicism and Protestantism have led the two camps to reconsider inadequate Reformation-generated formulations of this problem. This important book helped lay the groundwork for this badly needed task.

Thornton, L. S. *Revelation and the Modern World.* Westminster: Dacre Press, 1950. By firmly establishing the organic and necessary relationship between the form and content of God's revelation, this book effectively rebuts demythologizing and overcontextualizing approaches to the Bible and salvation history.

Torrance, Thomas F. *Theology in Reconciliation.* Grand Rapids: Eerdmans, 1976. The author's thesis is a most original and provocative one: The inability of the Western church to rid itself of dualistic metaphysics has led it into subtle disguised heresies (monophysitism) and fragmentation. The road to reconciliation is by way of recovering Athanasius' holistic metaphysics.

Turner, H. E. W. *The Pattern of Christian Truth.* London: Mowbrays, 1954. The continuing efforts of radical scholars to establish doctrinal discontinuity between the apostolic and patristic church are thoroughly confuted by this great book.

Underhill, Evelyn. *Worship.* London: Nisbet, 1943. Still one of the best introductions to the subject available, this book stresses that worship is rooted in ontology. Especially good is the discussion of the relationship of sacrifice and sacrament.

Vanauken, Sheldon. *A Severe Mercy.* San Francisco: Harper and Row, 1977. The importance of this book can scarcely be overestimated. One finishes it convinced that it represents a life vocation (though a unique and unexpected one) gloriously fulfilled.

Voll, Dieter. *Catholic Evangelicalism.* London: The Faith Press, 1963. Though evangelicalism and Catholicism were sundered at the Reformation, the ecumenical movement has sought to reunite them. This book investigates perhaps the only instance of the reuniting—which occurred in the English Church in the late nineteenth century—of these two necessary Christian principles.

Webber, Robert. *Common Roots.* Grand Rapids: Zondervan, 1978. American evangelicalism has finally received recognition as an important voice in Christendom. This significant book rightly contends that evangelicalism must mature if it is to realize its full potential.

Wells, David F. *Revolution in Rome.* Downers Grove: InterVarsity Press, 1972. This shrewd analysis of the apparent undermining of orthodoxy in post-Vatican II Rome perhaps lays too much stress on the influence of Catholic "progressives." Nevertheless, it is a valuable study of contemporary Roman Catholic thought.

Williams, Charles. *Descent of the Dove*. Grand Rapids: Eerdmans, 1976. W. H. Auden once said that he made a habit of rereading this book every year. If you can read only one history of the church, make sure it's this one.